PENGUIN BOOKS — GREAT IDEAS

Why I am So Wise

Friedrich Nietzsche

1844–1900

Friedrich Nietzsche

Why I am So Wise

TRANSLATED BY R. J. HOLLINGDALE

PENGUIN BOOKS — GREAT IDEAS

PENGUIN BOOKS

Published by the Penguin Group

Penguin Group (USA) Inc., 375 Hudson Street, New York, New York 10014, U.S.A.
Penguin Group (Canada), 90 Eglinton Avenue East, Suite 700, Toronto,
Ontario, Canada M4P 2Y3 (a division of Pearson Penguin Canada Inc.)
Penguin Books Ltd, 80 Strand, London WC2R 0RL, England
Penguin Ireland, 25 St Stephen's Green, Dublin 2, Ireland (a division of Penguin Books Ltd)
Penguin Group (Australia), 250 Camberwell Road, Camberwell,
Victoria 3124, Australia (a division of Pearson Australia Group Pty Ltd)
Penguin Books India Pvt Ltd, 11 Community Centre,
Panchsheel Park, New Delhi – 110 017, India
Penguin Group (NZ), cnr Airborne and Rosedale Roads, Albany, Auckland 1310, New
Zealand (a division of Pearson New Zealand Ltd)
Penguin Books (South Africa) (Pty) Ltd, 24 Sturdee Avenue,
Rosebank, Johannesburg 2196, South Africa

Penguin Books Ltd, Registered Offices: 80 Strand, London WC2R 0RL, England

Götzen-Dämmerung first published 1889
This translation first published in Penguin Classics 1968
Ecce Homo first published 1908
This translation first published in Penguin Classics 1979
Published in Penguin Books (U.K.) 2004
First published in the United States of America by Penguin Books 2005

3 5 7 9 10 8 6 4

Translations copyright © R. J. Hollingdale, 1968, 1979
All rights reserved

Taken from the Penguin Classics editions of *Ecce Homo* and
Twilight of the Idols/The Anti-Christ, translated by R. J. Hollingdale

LIBRARY OF CONGRESS CATALOGING IN PUBLICATION DATA
Nietzsche, Friedrich Wilhelm, 1844–1900.
[Götzendämmerung. English]
Why I am so wise / Friedrich Nietzsche ; translated by R. J. Hollingdale.
p.   cm.—(Great ideas)
ISBN 0 14 30.3634 3
1. Philosophy.   I. Title.   II. Series.
B3313.G6713 2005
193—dc22   2005047449

Printed in the United States of America
Set in Monotype Dante

Contents

Ecce Homo

How One Becomes What One Is

Foreword

SEEING that I must shortly approach mankind with the heaviest demand that has ever been made on it, it seems to me indispensable to say *who I am*. This ought really to be known already: for I have not neglected to 'bear witness' about myself. But the disparity between the greatness of my task and the *smallness* of my contemporaries has found expression in the fact that I have been neither heard nor even so much as seen. I live on my own credit, it is perhaps merely a prejudice that I am alive at all? . . . I need only to talk with any of the 'cultured people' who come to the Ober-Engadin in the summer to convince myself that I am *not* alive . . . Under these circumstances there exists a duty against which my habit, even more the pride of my instincts revolts, namely to say: *Listen to me! for I am thus and thus. Do not, above all, confound me with what I am not!*

2

I am, for example, absolutely not a bogey-man, not a moral-monster – I am even an antithetical nature to the species of man hitherto honoured as virtuous. Between ourselves, it seems to me that precisely this constitutes part of my pride. I am a disciple of the philosopher

Dionysos, I prefer to be even a satyr rather than a saint. But you have only to read this writing. Perhaps I have succeeded in giving expression to this antithesis in a cheerful and affable way – perhaps this writing had no point at all other than to do this. The last thing *I* would promise would be to 'improve' mankind. I erect no new idols; let the old idols learn what it means to have legs of clay. *To overthrow idols* (my word for 'ideals') – that rather is my business. Reality has been deprived of its value, its meaning, its veracity to the same degree as an ideal world has been *fabricated* . . . The 'real world' and the 'apparent world' – in plain terms: the *fabricated* world and reality . . . The *lie* of the ideal has hitherto been the curse on reality, through it mankind itself has become mendacious and false down to its deepest instincts – to the point of worshipping the *inverse* values to those which alone could guarantee it prosperity, future, the exalted *right* to a future.

3

He who knows how to breathe the air of my writings knows that it is an air of the heights, a *robust* air. One has to be made for it, otherwise there is no small danger one will catch cold. The ice is near, the solitude is terrible – but how peacefully all things lie in the light! how freely one breathes! how much one feels *beneath* one! – Philosophy, as I have hitherto understood and lived it, is a voluntary living in ice and high mountains – a seeking after everything strange and questionable in existence, all that has hitherto been excommunicated by morality. From the lengthy experience afforded by such a wandering in the *forbidden* I learned to view the origin of moralizing and idealizing very differently from what might be desirable: the *hidden* history of the philosophers, the psychology of their great names came to light for me. – How much truth can a spirit *bear*, how much truth can a spirit *dare*? that became for me more and more the real measure of value. Error (– belief in the ideal –) is not blindness, error is *cowardice* . . . Every acquisition, every step forward in knowledge is the *result* of courage, of severity towards oneself, of cleanliness with respect to oneself . . . I do not refute ideals, I merely draw on gloves in their presence . . . *Nitimur in* vetitum:* in this sign my philosophy will one day conquer, for what has hitherto been forbidden on principle has never been anything but the truth.–

4

– Within my writings my *Zarathustra* stands by itself. I have with this book given mankind the greatest gift that has ever been given it. With a voice that speaks across millennia, it is not only the most exalted book that exists, the actual book of the air of the heights – the entire fact man lies at a tremendous distance *beneath* it – it is also the *profoundest*, born out of the innermost abundance of truth, an inexhaustible well into which no bucket descends without coming up filled with gold and goodness. Here there speaks no 'prophet', none of those gruesome hybrids of sickness and will to power called founders of religions. One has above all to *hear* correctly

* 'We strive after the forbidden' (*Ovid*).

the tone that proceeds from this mouth, this halcyon tone, if one is not to do pitiable injustice to the meaning of its wisdom. 'It is the stillest words which bring the storm, thoughts that come on doves' feet guide the world –'

The figs are falling from the trees, they are fine and sweet: and as they fall their red skins split. I am a north wind to ripe figs.

Thus, like figs, do these teachings fall to you, my friends: now drink their juice and eat their sweet flesh! It is autumn all around and clear sky and afternoon –

Here there speaks no fanatic, here there is no 'preaching', here *faith* is not demanded: out of an infinite abundance of light and depth of happiness there falls drop after drop, word after word – a tender slowness of pace is the tempo of these discourses. Such things as this reach only the most select; it is an incomparable privilege to be a listener here; no one is free to have ears for Zarathustra . . . With all this, is Zarathustra not a *seducer*? . . . But what does he himself say when for the first time he again goes back into his solitude? Precisely the opposite of that which any sort of 'sage', 'saint', 'world-redeemer' and other *décadent* would say in such a case . . . He does not only speak differently, he *is* different . . .

I now go away alone, my disciples! You too now go away and be alone! So I will have it.

Go away from me and guard yourselves against Zarathustra! And better still: be ashamed of him! Perhaps he has deceived you.

The man of knowledge must be able not only to love his enemies but also to hate his friends.

One repays a teacher badly if one remains only a pupil. And why, then, should you not pluck at my laurels?

You respect me; but how if one day your respect should tumble? Take care that a falling statue does not strike you dead!

You say you believe in Zarathustra? But of what importance is Zarathustra? You are my believers: but of what importance are all believers?

You had not yet sought yourselves when you found me. Thus do all believers; therefore all belief is of so little account.

Now I bid you lose me and find yourselves; and only *when you have all denied me* will I return to you . . .

FRIEDRICH NIETZSCHE

On this perfect day, when everything has become ripe and not only the grapes are growing brown, a ray of sunlight has fallen on to my life: I looked behind me, I looked before me, never have I seen so many and such good things together. Not in vain have I buried my forty-fourth year today, I was *entitled* to bury it – what there was of life in it is rescued, is immortal. The first book of the *Revaluation of all Values*, the *Songs of Zarathustra*, the Twilight of the Idols, my attempt to philosophize with a hammer – all of them gifts of this year, of its last quarter even! *How should I not be grateful to my whole life?* – And so I tell myself my life.

Why I am So Wise

I

THE fortunateness of my existence, its uniqueness perhaps, lies in its fatality: to express it in the form of a riddle, as my father I have already died, as my mother I still live and grow old. This twofold origin, as it were from the highest and the lowest rung of the ladder of life, at once *décadent* and *beginning* – this if anything explains that neutrality, that freedom from party in relation to the total problem of life which perhaps distinguishes me. I have a subtler sense for signs of ascent and decline than any man has ever had, I am the teacher *par excellence* in this matter – I know both, I am both. – My father died at the age of thirty-six: he was delicate, lovable and morbid, like a being destined to pay this world only a passing visit – a gracious reminder of life rather than life itself. In the same year in which his life declined mine too declined: in the thirty-sixth year of my life I arrived at the lowest point of my vitality – I still lived, but without being able to see three paces in front of me. At that time – it was 1879 – I relinquished my Basel professorship, lived through the summer like a shadow in St Moritz and the following winter, the most sunless of my life, *as* a shadow in Naumburg. This was my minimum: 'The Wanderer and his Shadow' came into

9

existence during the course of it. I undoubtedly knew all about shadows in those days . . . In the following winter, the first winter I spent in Genoa, that sweetening and spiritualization which is virtually inseparable from an extreme poverty of blood and muscle produced 'Daybreak'. The perfect brightness and cheerfulness, even exuberance of spirit reflected in the said work is in my case compatible not only with the profoundest physiological weakness, but even with an extremity of pain. In the midst of the torments which attended an uninterrupted three-day headache accompanied by the laborious vomiting of phlegm – I possessed a dialectical clarity *par excellence* and thought my way very cold-bloodedly through things for which when I am in better health I am not enough of a climber, not refined, not *cold* enough. My readers perhaps know the extent to which I regard dialectics as a symptom of *décadence*, for example in the most famous case of all: in the case of Socrates. – All morbid disturbances of the intellect, even that semi-stupefaction consequent on fever, have remained to this day totally unfamiliar things to me, on their nature and frequency I had first to instruct myself by scholarly methods. My blood flows slowly. No one has ever been able to diagnose fever in me. A doctor who treated me for some time as a nervous case said at last: 'No! there is nothing wrong with your nerves, it is only I who am nervous.' Any kind of local degeneration absolutely undemonstrable; no organically originating stomach ailment, though there does exist, as a consequence of general exhaustion, a profound weakness of the gastric system. Condition of the eyes, sometimes approaching dangerously close to blindness, also only consequence, not causal: so that with every increase in vitality eyesight has also again improved. – Convalescence means with me a long, all too long succession of years – it also unfortunately means relapse, deterioration, periods of a kind of *décadence*. After all this do I need to say that in questions of *décadence* I am *experienced*? I have spelled it out forwards and backwards. Even that filigree art of grasping and comprehending in general, that finger for nuances, that psychology of 'looking around the corner' and whatever else characterizes me was learned only then, is the actual gift of that time in which everything in me became more subtle, observation itself together with all the organs of observation. To look from a morbid perspective towards *healthier* concepts and values, and again conversely to look down from the abundance and certainty of *rich* life into the secret labour of the instinct of *décadence* – that is what I have practised most, it has been my own particular field of experience, in this if in anything I am a master. I now have the skill and know-ledge to *invert perspectives*: first reason why a 'revaluation of values' is perhaps possible at all to me alone. –

2

Setting aside the fact that I am a *décadent*, I am also its antithesis. My proof of this is, among other things, that in combating my sick conditions I always instinctively chose the *right* means: while the *décadent* as such always chooses the means harmful to him. As *summa summarum* I was healthy, as corner, as speciality I was *décadent*. That energy for absolute isolation and detachment from my accustomed circumstances, the way I compelled myself no longer to let myself be cared for, served, *doctored* – this betrayed an unconditional certainty of instinct as to *what* at that time was needful above all else. I took myself in hand, I myself made myself healthy again: the precondition for this – every physiologist will admit it – is that *one is fundamentally healthy*. A being who is typically morbid cannot become healthy, still less can he make himself healthy; conversely, for one who is typically healthy being sick can even be an energetic *stimulant* to life, to more life. Thus in fact does that long period of sickness seem to me *now*: I discovered life as it were anew, myself included, I tasted all good and even petty things in a way that others could not easily taste them – I made out of my will to health, to *life*, my philosophy . . . For pay heed to this: it was in the years of my lowest vitality that I *ceased* to be a pessimist: the instinct for self-recovery *forbade* to me a philosophy of indigence and discouragement . . . And in what does one really recognize that someone has *turned out well*! In that a human being who has turned out well does our senses good: that he is carved out of wood at once hard, delicate and sweet-smelling. He has a taste only for what is beneficial to him; his pleasure, his joy ceases where the measure of what is beneficial is overstepped. He divines cures for injuries, he employs ill chances to his own advantage; what does not kill him makes him stronger. Out of everything he sees, hears, experiences he instinctively collects together *his* sum: he is a principle of selection, he rejects much. He is always in *his* company, whether he traffics with books, people or landscapes: he does honour when he *chooses*, when he *admits*, when he *trusts*. He reacts slowly to every kind of stimulus, with that slowness which a protracted caution and a willed pride have bred in him – he tests an approaching stimulus, he is far from going out to meet it. He believes in neither 'misfortune' nor in 'guilt': he knows how to *forget* – he is strong enough for everything to *have* to turn out for the best for him. Very well, I am the *opposite* of a *décadent*: for I have just described *myself*.

3

I consider the fact that I had such a father as a great privilege: the peasants he preached to – for, after he had lived for several years at the court of Altenburg, he was a preacher in his last years – said that the angels must look like he did. And with this I touch on the question of race. I am a pure-blooded Polish nobleman, in whom there is no drop of bad blood, least of all German. When I look for my profoundest opposite, the incalculable pettiness of the instincts, I always find my mother and my sister – to be related to such *canaille* would be a blasphemy against my divinity. The treatment I have received from my mother and my sister, up to the present moment, fills me with inexpressible horror: there is an absolutely hellish machine at work here, operating with infallible certainty at the precise moment when I am most vulnerable – at my highest moments . . . for then one needs all one's strength to counter such a poisonous viper . . . physiological contiguity renders such a *disharmonia praestabilita* possible . . . But I confess that the deepest objection to the 'Eternal Recurrence', my real idea from the abyss, is always my mother and my sister. – But even as a Pole I am a monstrous atavism. One would have to go back centuries to find this noblest of races that the earth has ever possessed in so instinctively pristine a degree as I present it. I have, against everything that is today called *noblesse*, a sovereign feeling of distinction – I wouldn't award to the young German Kaiser the honour of being my coachman. There is one single case where I acknowledge my equal – I recognize it with profound gratitude. Frau Cosima Wagner is by far the noblest nature; and, so that I shouldn't say one word too few, I say that Richard Wagner was by far the most closely related man to me . . . The rest is silence . . . All the prevalent notions of degrees of kinship are physiological nonsense in an unsurpassable measure. The Pope still deals today in this nonsense. One is least related to one's parents: it would be the most extreme sign of vulgarity to be related to one's parents. Higher natures have their origins infinitely farther back, and with them much had to be assembled, saved and hoarded. The great individuals are the oldest: I don't understand it, but Julius Caesar could be my father – or Alexander, this Dionysos incarnate . . . At the very moment that I am writing this the post brings me a Dionysos-head.

4

I have never understood the art of arousing enmity towards myself – this too I owe to my incomparable father – even when it seemed to me very worthwhile to do so. However unchristian it may seem, I am not even inimical towards myself, one may turn my life this way and that, one will only rarely, at bottom only once, discover signs that anyone has borne ill will towards me – perhaps, however, somewhat too many signs of *good* will . . . My experiences even of those of whom everyone has bad experiences speak without exception in their favour; I tame every bear, I even make buffoons mind their manners. During the seven years in which I taught Greek to the top form of the Basel grammar school I never once had occasion to mete out a punishment; the laziest were industrious when they were with me. I am always up to dealing with any chance event; I have to be unprepared if I am to be master of myself. Let the instrument be what it will, let it be as out of tune as only the instrument 'man' can become out of tune – I should have to be ill not to succeed in getting out of it something listenable. And how often have I heard from the 'instruments' themselves that they had never heard themselves sound so well . . . Most beautifully perhaps from that Heinrich von Stein who died so unpardonably young and who, after cautiously obtaining permission, once appeared for three days at Sils-Maria, explaining to everyone that he had *not* come for the Engadin. This excellent man, who with the whole impetuous artlessness of a Prussian Junker had waded into the Wagnerian swamp (– and into the swamp of Dühring in addition!), was during those three days as if transported by a storm-wind of freedom, like one suddenly raised to *his own* heights and given wings. I kept telling him it was the result of the fine air up here, that everyone felt the same, that you could not stand 6,000 feet above Bayreuth and not notice it – but he would not believe me . . . If, this notwithstanding, many great and petty misdeeds have been committed against me, it was not 'will', least of all *ill* will that was the cause of it: I could complain, rather – I have just suggested as much – of the good will which has caused me no little mischief in my life. My experiences give me a right to a general mistrust of the so-called 'selfless' drives, of the whole 'love of one's neighbour' which is always ready with deeds and advice. It counts with me as weakness, as a special case of the incapacity to withstand stimuli – it is only among *décadents* that *pity* is called a virtue. My reproach against those who practise pity is that shame, reverence, a delicate feeling for distance easily eludes them, that pity instantly smells of mob and is so like bad manners as to be mistaken for them – that the hands of pity can under certain circumstances intrude downright destructively into a great destiny, into a solitariness where wounds are nursed, into a *privilege* for great guilt. I count the overcoming of pity among the *noble* virtues: I have, as 'Zarathustra's Temptation', invented a case in which a great cry of distress reaches him, in which pity like an ultimate sin seeks to attack him, to seduce him from allegiance to *himself*. To remain master here, here to keep the *elevation* of one's task clean of the many lower and more shortsighted drives which are active in so-called selfless actions, that is the test, the final test perhaps, which a Zarathustra has to pass – the actual *proof* of his strength . . .

5

In yet another point I am merely my father once more and as it were the continuation of his life after an all too early death. Like anyone who has never lived among his equals and to whom the concept 'requital' is as inaccessible as is for instance the concept 'equal rights', I forbid myself in cases where a little or *very great* act of folly has been perpetrated against me any counter-measure, any protective measure – also, as is reasonable, any defence, any 'justification'. My kind of requital con-sists in sending after the piece of stupidity as quickly as possible a piece of sagacity: in that way one may perhaps overtake it. To speak in a metaphor. I dispatch a pot of jam to get rid of a *sour* affair . . . Let anyone harm me in any way, I 'requite' it, you may be sure of that: as soon as I can I find an opportunity of expressing my thanks to the 'offender' (occasionally even for the offence) – or of *asking* him for something, which can be more courteous than giving something . . . It also seems to me that the rudest word, the rudest letter are more good-natured, more honest than silence. Those who keep silent almost always lack subtlety and politeness of the heart; silence is an objection, swallowing down necessarily produces a bad character – it even ruins the stomach. All those given to silence are dyspeptic. – One will see that I would not like to see rudeness undervalued, it is the *most humane* form of contradiction by far and, in the midst of modern tendermindedness, one of our foremost virtues. – If one is rich enough, it is even fortunate to be in the wrong. A god come to earth ought to *do* nothing whatever but wrong: to take upon oneself, not the punishment, but the *guilt* – only that would be godlike.

6

Freedom from *ressentiment*, enlightenment over *ressentiment* – who knows the extent to which I ultimately owe thanks to my protracted sickness for this too! The problem is not exactly simple: one has to have experienced it from a state of strength and a state of weakness. If anything whatever has to be admitted against being sick, being weak, it is that in these conditions the actual curative instinct, that is to say the *defensive and offensive instinct* in man becomes soft. One does not know how to get free of anything, one does not know how to have done with anything, one does not know how to thrust back – everything hurts. Men and things come importunately close, events strike too deep, the memory is a festering wound. Being sick *is* itself a kind of *ressentiment*. – Against this the invalid has only one great means of cure – I call it *Russian fatalism*, that fatalism without rebellion with which a Russian soldier for whom the campaign has become too much at last lies down in the snow. No longer to take anything at all, to receive anything, to take anything *into* oneself – no longer to react at all . . . The great rationality of this fatalism, which is not always the courage to die but can be life-preservative under conditions highly dangerous to life, is reduction of the metabolism, making it slow down, a kind of will to hibernation. A couple of steps further in this logic and one has the fakir who sleeps for weeks on end in a grave . . . Because one would use oneself up too quickly *if* one reacted at all, one no longer reacts: this is the logic. And nothing burns one up quicker than the affects of *ressentiment*. Vexation, morbid susceptibility, incapacity for revenge, the desire, the thirst for revenge, poison-brewing in any sense – for one who is exhausted this is certainly the most disadvantageous kind of reaction: it causes a rapid expenditure of nervous energy, a morbid accretion of excretions, for example of gall into the stomach. *Ressentiment* is the forbidden *in itself* for the invalid – *his* evil: unfortunately also his most natural inclination. – This was grasped by that profound physiologist Buddha. His 'religion', which one would do better to call a *system of hygiene* so as not to mix it up with such pitiable things as Christianity, makes its effect dependent on victory over *ressentiment*: to free the soul of *that* – first step to recovery. 'Not by enmity is enmity ended, by friendship is enmity ended': this stands at the beginning of Buddha's teaching – it is *not* morality that speaks thus, it is physiology that speaks thus. – *Ressentiment*, born of weakness, to no one more harmful than to the weak man himself – in the opposite case, where a rich nature is the presupposition, a *superfluous* feeling to stay master of which is almost the proof of richness. He who knows the seriousness with which my philosophy has taken up the struggle against the feelings of vengefulness and vindictiveness even into the theory of 'free will' – my struggle against Christianity is only a special instance of it – will understand why it is precisely here that I throw the light on my personal bearing, my *sureness of instinct* in practice. In periods of *décadence* I *forbade* them to myself as harmful; as soon as life was again sufficiently rich and proud for them I forbade them to myself as *beneath* me. That 'Russian fatalism' of which I spoke came forward in my case in the form of clinging tenaciously for years on end to almost intolerable situations, places, residences, company, once chance had placed me in them – it was better than changing them, than *feeling* them as capable of being changed – than rebelling against them . . . In those days I took it deadly amiss if I was disturbed in this fatalism, if I was forcibly awakened from it – and to do this was in fact every time a deadly dangerous thing. – To accept oneself as a fate, not to desire oneself 'different' – in such conditions this is *great rationality* itself.

7

War is another thing. I am by nature warlike. To attack is among my instincts. *To be able* to be an enemy, to be an enemy – that perhaps presupposes a strong nature, it is in any event a condition of every strong nature. It needs resistances, consequently it *seeks* resistances: the *aggressive* pathos belongs as necessarily to strength as the feeling of vengefulness and vindictiveness does to weakness. Woman, for example, is vengeful: that is conditioned by her weakness, just as is her susceptibility to others' distress. – The strength of one who attacks has in the opposition he needs a kind of *gauge*; every growth reveals itself in the seeking out of a powerful opponent – or problem: for a philosopher who is warlike also challenges problems to a duel. The undertaking is to master, *not* any resistances that happen to present them-selves, but those against which one has to bring all one's strength, suppleness and mastery of weapons – to master *equal* opponents . . . Equality in face of the enemy – first presupposition of an *honest* duel. Where one despises one *cannot* wage war; where one commands, where one sees something as beneath one, one *has* not to wage war. – My practice in warfare can be reduced to four propositions. Firstly: I attack only causes that are victorious – under certain circumstances I wait until they are victorious. Secondly: I attack only causes against which I would find no allies, where I stand alone – where I compromise only myself . . . I have never taken a step in public which was not compromising: that is *my* criterion of right action. Thirdly: I never attack persons – I only employ the person as a strong magnifying glass with which one can make visible a general but furtive state of distress which is hard to get hold of. That was how I attacked David Strauss, more precisely the *success* with German 'culture' of a senile book – I thus caught that culture red-handed . . . That was how I attacked Wagner, more precisely the falseness, the hybrid instincts of our 'culture' which confuses the artful with the rich, the late with the great. Fourthly: I attack only things where any kind of personal difference is excluded, where there is no background of bad experience. On the contrary, to attack is with me a proof of good will, under certain circumstances of gratitude. I do honour, I confer distinction when I associate my name with a cause, a person: for or against – that is in this regard a matter of indifference to me. If I wage war on Christianity I have a right to do so, because I have never experienced anything disagreeable or frustrating from that direction – the most serious Christians have always been well disposed towards me. I myself, an opponent of Christianity *de rigueur*, am far from bearing a grudge against the individual for what is the fatality of millennia. –

8

May I venture to indicate one last trait of my nature which creates for me no little difficulty in my relations with others? I possess a perfectly uncanny sensitivity of the instinct for cleanliness, so that I perceive physiologically – *smell* – the proximity or – what am I saying? – the innermost parts, the 'entrails', of every soul . . . I have in this sensitivity psychological antennae with which I touch and take hold of every secret: all the *concealed* dirt at the bottom of many a nature, perhaps conditioned by bad blood but whitewashed by education, is known to me almost on first contact. If I have observed correctly, such natures unendurable to my sense of cleanliness for their part also sense the caution of my disgust: they do not thereby become any sweeter-smelling . . . As has always been customary with me – an extreme cleanliness in relation to me is a presupposition of my existence, I perish under unclean conditions – I swim and bathe and splash continually as it were in water, in any kind of perfectly transparent and glittering element. This makes traffic with people no small test of my patience; my humanity consists, *not* in feeling for and with man, but in *enduring* that I do feel for and with him . . . My humanity is a continual self-overcoming. – But I have need of *solitude*, that is to say recovery, return to myself, the breath of a free light playful air . . . My entire Zarathustra is a dithyramb on solitude or, if I have been understood, on *cleanliness* . . . Fortunately not on *pure folly*. – He who has eyes for colours will call it diamond. – *Disgust* at mankind, at the 'rabble', has always been my greatest danger . . . Do you want to hear the words in which Zarathustra speaks of *redemption* from disgust?

Yet what happened to me? How did I free myself from disgust? Who rejuvenated my eyes? How did I fly to the height where the rabble no longer sit at the well?

Did my disgust itself create wings and water-diving powers for me? Truly, I had to fly to the extremest height to find again the fountain of delight!

Oh, I have found it, my brothers! Here, in the extremest height, the fountain of delight gushes up for me! And here there is a life at which no rabble drinks with me!

You gush up almost too impetuously, fountain of delight! And in wanting to fill the cup, you often empty it again.

And I still have to learn to approach you more discreetly: my heart still flows towards you all too impetuously:–

my heart, upon which my summer burns, a short, hot, melancholy, over-joyful summer: how my summer-heart longs for your coolness!

Gone is the lingering affliction of my spring! Gone the snowflakes of my malice in June! Summer have I become entirely, and summer-noonday –

– a summer at the extremest height with cold

fountains and blissful stillness: oh come, my friends, that the stillness may become more blissful yet!

For this is *our* height and our home: we live too nobly and boldly here for all unclean men and their thirsts.

Only cast your pure eyes into the well of my delight, friends! You will not dim its sparkle! It shall laugh back at you with *its* purity.

We build our nest in the tree Future: eagles shall bring food to us solitaries in their beaks!

Truly, food in which no unclean men could join us! They would think they were eating fire and burn their mouths.

Truly, we do not prepare a home here for unclean men! Their bodies and their spirits would call our happiness a cave of ice!

So let us live above them like strong winds, neighbours of the eagles, neighbours of the snow, neighbours of the sun: that is how strong winds live.

And like a wind will I one day blow among them and with my spirit take away the breath of their spirit: thus my future will have it.

Truly, Zarathustra is a strong wind to all flatlands; and he offers this advice to his enemies and to all that spews and spits: take care not to spit *against* the wind! . . .

Why I am So Clever

WHY do I know a few *more* things? Why am I so clever altogether? I have never reflected on questions that are none – I have not squandered myself. – I have, for example, no experience of actual *religious* difficulties. I am entirely at a loss to know to what extent I ought to have felt 'sinful'. I likewise lack a reliable criterion of a pang of conscience: from what one *hears* of it, a pang of conscience does not seem to me anything respectable . . . I should not like to leave an act in the lurch *afterwards*, I would as a matter of principle prefer to leave the evil outcome, the *consequences*, out of the question of values. When the outcome is evil one can easily lose the *true* eye for what one has done: a pang of conscience seems to me a kind of '*evil* eye'. To honour to oneself something that went wrong all the more *because* it went wrong – that rather would accord with my morality. – 'God', 'immortality of the soul', 'redemption', 'the Beyond', all of them concepts to which I have given no attention and no time, not even as a child – perhaps I was never childish enough for it? – I have absolutely no knowledge of atheism as an outcome of reasoning, still less as an event: with me it is obvious by instinct. I am too inquisitive, too *questionable*, too high spirited to rest content with a crude answer. God is a crude answer, a piece of indelicacy against us thinkers – fundamentally even a crude *prohibition* to us: you shall not think! . . . I am interested in quite a different way in a question upon which the 'salvation of mankind' depends far more than it does upon any kind of quaint curiosity of the theologians: the question of *nutriment*. One can for convenience' sake formulate it thus: 'how to nourish yourself so as to attain your maximum of strength, of *virtù* in the Renaissance style, of moraline-free virtue?' – My experiences here are as bad as they possibly could be; I am astonished that I heard this question so late, that I learned 'reason' from these experiences so late. Only the perfect worthlessness of our German education – its 'idealism' – can to some extent explain to me why on precisely this point I was backward to the point of holiness. This 'education' which from the first teaches one to lose sight of *realities* so as to hunt after altogether problematic, so-called 'ideal' objectives, 'classical education' for example – as if it were not from the first an utterly fruitless undertaking to try to unite 'classical' and 'German' in *one* concept! It is, moreover, mirth-provoking – just think of a 'classically educated' Leipziger! – Until my very maturest years I did in fact eat *badly* – in the language of morals 'impersonally', 'selflessly', 'altruistically', for the salvation of cooks and other fellow Christians. With the aid of Leipzig cookery, for example, which accompanied my earliest study of Schopenhauer (1865), I very earnestly denied my 'will to live'. To ruin one's stomach so as to receive inadequate nutriment – the aforesaid cookery seems to me to solve this problem wonderfully well. But German

cookery in general – what does it not have on its conscience! Soup *before* the meal (in Venetian cookery books
of the sixteenth century still called *alla tedesca*); meat
cooked to shreds, greasy and floury vegetables; the
degeneration of puddings to paperweights! If one adds
to this the downright bestial dinner-drinking habits of
the ancient and by no means only the *ancient* Germans
one will also understand the origin of the *German spirit*
– disturbed intestines . . . The German spirit is an indiges-
tion, it can have done with nothing. – But to the *English*
diet too, which compared with the Germans, even with
the French, is a kind of 'return to nature', that is to say
to cannibalism, my own instinct is profoundly opposed;
it seems to me to give the spirit *heavy* feet – the feet of
Englishwomen . . . The best cookery is that of *Piedmont*.
Alcoholic drinks are no good for me; a glass of wine or
beer a day is quite enough to make life for me a 'Vale of
Tears' – Munich is where my antipodes live. Granted I
was a little late to grasp this – I *experienced* it really from
childhood onwards. As a boy I believed wine-drinking
to be, like tobacco-smoking, at first only a vanity of
young men, later a habit. Perhaps the wine of Naumburg
is in part to blame for this *austere* judgement. To believe
that wine *makes cheerful* I would have to be a Christian,
that is to say believe what is for precisely me an absurdity.
Oddly enough, while I am put extremely out of sorts by
small, much diluted doses of alcohol, I am almost turned
into a sailor when it comes to *strong* doses. Even as a
boy I showed how brave I was in this respect. To write
a long Latin essay in a *single* night's sitting and then go
on to make a fair copy of it, with the ambition in my

pen to imitate in severity and concision my model Sallust, and to pour a quantity of grog of the heaviest calibre over my Latin, was even when I was a pupil of venerable Schulpforta in no way opposed to my physiology, nor perhaps to that of Sallust – however much it might have been to venerable Schulpforta . . . Later, towards the middle of life, I decided, to be sure, more and more strictly *against* any sort of 'spirituous' drink: an opponent of vegetarianism from experience, just like Richard Wagner, who converted me, I cannot advise all *more spiritual* natures too seriously to abstain from alcohol absolutely. *Water* suffices . . . I prefer places in which there is everywhere opportunity to drink from flowing fountains (Nice, Turin, Sils); a small glass runs after me like a dog. *In vino veritas*: it seems that here too I am again at odds with all the world over the concept 'truth' – with me the spirit moves over the water . . . A couple more signposts from my morality. A big meal is easier to digest than one too small. That the stomach comes into action as a whole, first precondition of a good digestion. One has to *know* the size of one's stomach. For the same reason those tedious meals should be avoided which I call interrupted sacrificial feasts, those at the *table d'hôte*. – No eating between meals, no coffee: coffee makes gloomy. *Tea* beneficial only in the morning. Little, but strong: tea very detrimental and sicklying o'er the whole day if it is the slightest bit too weak. Each has here his own degree, often between the narrowest and most delicate limits. In a very *agaçant* climate it is inadvisable to start with tea: one should start an hour earlier with a cup of thick oil-free cocoa. – *Sit* as little as possible;

credit no thought not born in the open air and while moving freely about – in which the muscles too do not hold a festival. All prejudices come from the intestines. – Assiduity – I have said it once before – the actual *sin* against the holy spirit. –

2

Most closely related to the question of nutriment is the question of *place* and *climate*. No one is free to live everywhere; and he who has great tasks to fulfil which challenge his entire strength has indeed in this matter a very narrow range of choice. The influence of climate on the *metabolism*, its slowing down, its speeding up, extends so far that a blunder in regard to place and climate can not only estrange anyone from his task but withhold it from him altogether: he never catches sight of it. His animalic *vigor* never grows sufficiently great for him to attain to that freedom overflowing into the most spiritual domain where he knows: *that* I alone can do . . . A never so infinitesimal sluggishness of the intestines grown into a bad habit completely suffices to transform a genius into something mediocre, something 'German'; the German climate alone is enough to discourage strong and even heroic intestines. The *tempo* of the metabolism stands in an exact relationship to the mobility or lameness of the *feet* of the spirit; the 'spirit' itself is indeed only a species of this metabolism. Make a list of the places where there are and have been gifted men, where wit, refinement, malice are a part of happiness, where genius has almost necessarily made its home: they all possess an excellent dry air. Paris, Provence, Florence, Jerusalem,

Athens – these names prove something: that genius is *conditioned* by dry air, clear sky – that is to say by rapid metabolism, by the possibility of again and again supplying oneself with great, even tremendous quantities of energy. I have in mind a case in which a spirit which might have become significant and free became instead narrow, withdrawn, a grumpy specialist, merely through a lack of instinctive subtlety in choice of climate. And I myself could in the end have become this case if sickness had not compelled me to reason, to reflect on reason in reality. Now, when from long practice I read climatic and meteorological effects off from myself as from a very delicate and reliable instrument and even on a short journey, from Turin to Milan for instance, verify on myself physiologically the change in degrees of humidity, I recall with horror the *uncanny* fact that my life up to the last ten years, the years when my life was in danger, was spent nowhere but in wrong places downright *forbidden* to me. Naumburg, Schulpforta, Thuringia in general, Leipzig, Basel, Venice – so many ill-fated places for my physiology. If I have no welcome memories at all of my whole childhood and youth, it would be folly to attribute this to so-called 'moral' causes – the undeniable lack of *adequate* company, for instance: for this lack exists today as it has always existed without preventing me from being brave and cheerful. Ignorance *in physiologis* – accursed 'idealism' – is the real fatality in my life, the superfluous and stupid in it, something out of which nothing good grows, for which there is no compensation, no counter-reckoning. It is as a consequence of this 'idealism' that I elucidate to myself all the blunders, all the great deviations of instinct and 'modesties' which led me away from the *task* of my life, that I became a philologist for example – why not at least a physician or something else that opens the eyes? In my time at Basel my entire spiritual diet, the division of the day included, was a perfectly senseless abuse of extraordinary powers without any kind of provision for covering this consumption, without even reflection on consumption and replacement. Any more subtle selfishness, any *protection* by a commanding instinct was lacking, it was an equating of oneself with everyone else, a piece of 'selflessness', a forgetting of one's distance – something I shall never forgive myself. When I was almost done for, *because* I was almost done for, I began to reflect on this fundamental irrationality of my life – 'idealism'. It was only *sickness* that brought me to reason. –

3

Selectivity in nutriment; selectivity in climate and place; – the third thing in which one may at no cost commit a blunder is selectivity in *one's kind of recreation*. Here too the degree to which a spirit is *sui generis* makes ever narrower the bounds of what is permitted, that is to say *useful* to him. In my case all reading is among my recreations: consequently among those things which free me from myself, which allow me to saunter among strange sciences and souls – which I no longer take seriously. It is precisely reading which helps me to recover from *my* seriousness. At times when I am deeply sunk in work you will see no books around me: I would guard against letting anyone speak or even think in my vicinity. And that is what reading would mean . . . Has it really been noticed that in that state of profound tension to which pregnancy condemns the spirit and fundamentally the entire organism, any chance event, any kind of stimulus from without has too vehement an effect, 'cuts' too deeply? One has to avoid the chance event, the stimulus from without, as much as possible; a kind of self-walling-up is among the instinctual sagacities of spiritual pregnancy. Shall I allow a *strange* thought to climb secretly over the wall? – And that is what reading would mean . . . The times of work and fruitfulness are followed by the time of recreation: come hither, you pleasant, you witty, you clever books! Will they be German books? . . . I have to reckon back half a year to catch myself with a book in my hand. But what was it? – An excellent study by Victor Brochard, *les sceptiques Grecs*, in which my Laertiana are also well employed. The Sceptics, the only *honourable* type among the two- and five-fold ambiguous philosophical crowd! . . . Otherwise I take flight almost always to the same books, really a small number, those books which have *proved* themselves precisely to me. It does not perhaps lie in my nature to read much or many kinds of things: a reading room makes me ill. Neither does it lie in my nature to love much or many kinds of things. Caution, even hostility towards new books is rather part of my instinct than 'tolerance', '*largeur du coeur*' and other forms of 'neighbour love' . . . It is really only a small number of older Frenchmen to whom I return again and again: I believe only in French culture and consider everything in Europe that calls itself 'culture' a misunderstanding, not to speak of German culture . . . The few instances of high culture I have encountered in Germany have all been of French origin, above all Frau Cosima Wagner, by far the first voice I have heard in questions of taste. – That I do not read Pascal but *love* him, as the most instructive of all sacrifices to Christianity, slowly murdered first physically then psychologically, the whole logic of this most horrible form of inhuman cruelty; that I have something of Montaigne's wantonness in my spirit, who knows? perhaps also in my body; that my artist's taste defends the names Molière, Corneille and Racine, not without wrath, against a disorderly genius such as Shakespeare: this does not ultimately exclude my finding the most recent Frenchmen also charming company. I cannot at all conceive in which century of history one could haul together such inquisitive and at the same time such delicate psychologists as one can in contemporary Paris: I name as a sample – for their number is by no means small, Messrs Paul Bourget, Pierre Loti, Gyp, Meilhac, Anatole France, Jules Lemaitre, or to pick out one of the stronger race, a genuine Latin to whom I am especially attached, Guy de Maupassant. Between ourselves, I prefer *this* generation even to their great teachers, who have all been ruined by German philosophy (M. Taine for example by Hegel, whom he has to thank for this misunderstanding of great human beings and ages). As far as Germany extends it *ruins* culture. It was only the war that 'redeemed' the spirit in France . . . Stendhal, one of the fairest accidents of my life – for whatever marks an epoch in my life has been brought to me by accident, never by a recommendation – is utterly invaluable with his anticipating psychologist's eye, with his grasp of facts which reminds one of the proximity of the greatest man of the factual (*ex ungue Napoleonem* –); finally not least as an *honest* atheist, a rare, almost undiscoverable species in France – with all deference to *Prosper Mérimée* . . . Perhaps I am even envious of Stendhal? He robbed me of the best atheist joke which precisely I could have made: 'God's only excuse is that he does not exist' . . . I myself have said somewhere: what has hitherto been the greatest objection to existence? *God* . . .

4

The highest conception of the lyric poet was given me by *Heinrich Heine*. I seek in vain in all the realms of millennia for an equally sweet and passionate music. He possesses that divine malice without which I cannot imagine perfection – I assess the value of people, of races according to how necessarily they are unable to separate the god from the satyr. – And how he employs German! It will one day be said that Heine and I have been by far the first artists of the German language – at an incalculable distance from everything which mere Germans have done with it. – I must be profoundly related to *Byron's* Manfred: I discovered all these abysses in myself – I was ripe for this work at thirteen. I have no words, only a look for those who dare to say the word Faust in the presence of Manfred. The Germans are *incapable* of any conception of greatness: proof Schumann. Expressly from wrath against this sugary Saxon, I composed a counter-overture to Manfred, of which Hans von Bülow said he had never seen the like on manuscript paper: it constituted a rape on Euterpe. – When I seek my highest formula for *Shakespeare* I find it always in that he conceived the type of Caesar. One cannot guess at things like this – one is it or one is not. The great poet creates *only* out of his own reality – to the point at which he is afterwards unable to endure his own work . . . When I have taken a glance at my Zarathustra I walk up and down my room for half an hour unable to master an unendurable spasm of sobbing. – I know of no more heartrending reading than Shakespeare: what must a man have suffered to need to be a buffoon to this extent! – Is Hamlet *understood*? It is not doubt, it is *certainty* which makes mad . . . But to feel in this way one must be profound, abyss, philosopher . . . We all *fear* truth . . . And, to confess it: I am instinctively certain that Lord Bacon is the originator, the self-tormentor of this uncanniest species of literature: what do *I* care about the pitiable charter of American shallow-pates and muddle-heads? But the power for the mightiest reality of vision is not only compatible with the mightiest power for action, for the monstrous in action, for crime – *it even presupposes it* . . . We do not know nearly enough about Lord Bacon, the first realist in every great sense of the word, to know *what* he did, *what* he wanted, *what* he experienced within himself . . . And the devil take it, my dear critics! Supposing I had baptized my Zarathustra with another name, for example with the name of Richard Wagner, the perspicuity of two millennia would not have sufficed to divine that the author of 'Human, All Too Human' is the visionary of Zarathustra . . .

5

Here where I am speaking of the recreations of my life, I need to say a word to express my gratitude for that which of all things in it has refreshed me by far the most profoundly and cordially. This was without any doubt my intimate association with Richard Wagner. I offer all my other human relationships cheap; but at no price would I relinquish from my life the Tribschen days, those days of mutual confidences, of cheerfulness, of sublime incidents – of *profound* moments . . . I do not know what others may have experienced with Wagner: over *our* sky no cloud ever passed. – And with that I return again to France – I cannot spare reasons, I can spare a mere curl of the lip for Wagnerians *et hoc genus omne* who believe they are doing honour to Wagner when they find him similar to *themselves* . . . Constituted as I am, a stranger in my deepest instincts to everything German, so that the mere presence of a German hinders my digestion, my first contact with Wagner was also the first time in my life I ever drew a deep breath: I felt, I reverenced him as a being from *outside*, as the opposite, the incarnate protest against all 'German virtues'. – We who were children in the swamp-air of the fifties are necessarily pessimists regarding the concept 'German'; we cannot be anything but revolutionaries – we shall acquiesce in no state of things in which the *bigot* is on top. It is a matter of complete indifference to me if today he plays in different colours, if he dresses in scarlet and dons the uniform of a hussar . . . Very well Wagner was a revolutionary – he fled from the Germans . . . As an *artist* one has no home in Europe except in Paris: the *delicatesse* in all five senses of art which Wagner's art presupposes, the fingers for nuances, the psychological morbidity, is to be found only in Paris. Nowhere else does there exist such a passion in questions of form, this seriousness in *mise en scène* – it is the Parisian seriousness *par excellence*. There is in Germany absolutely no conception of the tremendous ambition which dwells in the soul of a Parisian artist. The German is good-natured – Wagner was by no means good-natured . . . But I have already said sufficient as to where Wagner belongs, in whom he has his closest relatives: the French late romantics, that high-flying and yet exhilarating kind of artists such as Delacroix, such as Berlioz, with a *fond* of sickness, of incurability in their nature, sheer fanatics for *expression*, virtuosi through and through . . . Who was the first *intelligent* adherent of Wagner? Charles Baudelaire, the same as was the first to understand Delacroix, that typical *décadent* in whom an entire race of artists recognized themselves – he was perhaps also the last . . . What I have never forgiven Wagner? That he *condescended* to the Germans – that he became *reichsdeutsch* . . . As far as Germany extends it *ruins* culture. –

6

All in all I could not have endured my youth without Wagnerian music. For I was *condemned* to Germans. If one wants to get free from an unendurable pressure one needs hashish. Very well, I needed Wagner. Wagner is the counter-poison to everything German *par excellence* – still poison, I do not dispute it . . . From the moment

37

there was a piano score of Tristan – my compliments, Herr von Bülow! – I was a Wagnerian. The earliest works of Wagner I saw as beneath me – still too common, too 'German' . . . But I still today seek a work of a dangerous fascination, of a sweet and shuddery infinity equal to that of Tristan – I seek in all the arts in vain. All the strangenesses of Leonardo da Vinci lose their magic at the first note of Tristan. This work is altogether Wagner's *non plus ultra*; he recuperated from it with the Meistersinger and the Ring. To become healthier – that is *retrogression* in the case of a nature such as Wagner . . . I take it for a piece of good fortune of the first rank to have lived at the right time, and to have lived precisely among Germans, so as to be *ripe* for this work: my psychologist's inquisitiveness goes that far. The world is poor for him who has never been sick enough for this 'voluptuousness of hell': to employ a mystic's formula is permissible, almost obligatory, here. I think I know better than anyone what tremendous things Wagner was capable of, the fifty worlds of strange delights to which no one but he had wings; and as I am strong enough to turn even the most questionable and most perilous things to my own advantage and thus to become stronger, I call Wagner the great benefactor of my life. That in which we are related, that we have suffered more profoundly, from one another also, than men of this century are capable of suffering, will eternally join our names together again and again; and as surely as Wagner is among Germans merely a misunderstanding, just as surely am I and always will be. – Two centuries of psychological and artistic discipline *first*, my Herr Germans! . . . But one cannot catch up that amount. –

7

I shall say another word for the most select ears: what I really want from music. That it is cheerful and profound, like an afternoon in October. That it is individual, wanton, tender, a little sweet woman of lowness and charm . . . I shall never admit that a German *could* know what music is. What one calls German musicians, the greatest above all, are *foreigners*, Slavs, Croats, Italians, Netherlanders – or Jews: otherwise Germans of the strong race, *extinct* Germans, like Heinrich Schütz, Bach and Handel. I myself am still sufficient of a Pole to exchange the rest of music for Chopin; for three reasons I exclude Wagner's Siegfried Idyll, perhaps also a few things by Liszt, who excels all other musicians in the nobility of his orchestral tone; finally all that has grown up beyond the Alps – *this side* . . . I would not know how to get on without Rossini, even less without *my* south in music, the music of my Venetian *maestro Pietro Gasti*. And when I say beyond the Alps I am really saying only Venice. When I seek another word for music I never find any other word than Venice. I do not know how to distinguish between tears and music – I do not know how to think of happiness, of the *south*, without a shudder of faintheartedness.

> Lately I stood at the bridge
> in the brown night.
> From afar there came a song:
> a golden drop, it swelled

across the trembling surface.
Gondolas, lights, music –
drunken it swam out into the gloom . . .
My soul, a stringed instrument,
touched by invisible hands
sang to itself in reply a gondola song,
and trembled with gaudy happiness.
– Was anyone listening?

8

In all this – in selection of nutriment, of place and
climate, of recreation – there commands an instinct of
self-preservation which manifests itself most unambigu-
ously as an instinct for *self-defence*. Not to see many
things, not to hear them, not to let them approach one
– first piece of ingenuity, first proof that one is no
accident but a necessity. The customary word for this
self-defensive instinct is *taste*. Its imperative commands,
not only to say No when Yes would be a piece of
'selflessness', but also to say *No as little as possible*. To
separate oneself, to depart from that to which No would
be required again and again. The rationale is that defensive expenditures, be they never so small, become a
rule, a habit, lead to an extraordinary and perfectly
superfluous impoverishment. Our *largest* expenditures
are our most frequent small ones. Warding off, not
letting come close, is an expenditure – one should not
deceive oneself over this – a strength *squandered* on
negative objectives. One can merely through the con-
stant need to ward off become too weak any longer to

defend oneself. – Suppose I were to step out of my house and discover, instead of calm and aristocratic Turin, the German provincial town: my instinct would have to blockade itself so as to push back all that pressed upon it from this flat and cowardly world. Or suppose I discovered the German metropolis, that builded vice where nothing grows, where every kind of thing, good and bad, is dragged in. Would I not in face of it have to become a *hedgehog*? – But to have spikes is an extravagance, a double luxury even if one is free to have no spikes but *open* hands . . .

Another form of sagacity and self-defence consists in *reacting as seldom as possible* and withdrawing from situations and relationships in which one would be condemned as it were to suspend one's 'freedom', one's initiative, and become a mere reagent. I take as a parable traffic with books. The scholar, who really does nothing but 'trundle' books – the philologist at a modest assessment about 200 a day – finally loses altogether the ability to think for himself. If he does not trundle he does not think. He *replies* to a stimulus (– a thought he has read) when he thinks – finally he does nothing but react. The scholar expends his entire strength in affirmation and denial, in criticizing what has already been thought – he himself no longer thinks . . . The instinct for self-defence has in his case become soft; otherwise he would defend himself against books. The scholar – a *décadent*. – This I have seen with my own eyes: natures gifted, rich and free already in their thirties 'read to ruins', mere matches that have to be struck if they are to ignite – emit 'thoughts'. – Early in the morning at the break of day, in all the freshness and dawn of one's strength, to read a *book* – I call that vicious! –

9

At this point I can no longer avoid actually answering the question *how one becomes what one is*. And with that I touch on the masterpiece in the art of self-preservation – of *selfishness* ... For assuming that the task, the vocation, the *destiny* of the task exceeds the average measure by a significant degree, there would be no greater danger than to catch sight of oneself *with* this task. That one becomes what one is presupposes that one does not have the remotest idea *what* one is. From this point of view even the *blunders* of life – the temporary sidepaths and wrong turnings, the delays, the 'modesties', the seriousness squandered on tasks which lie outside *the* task – have their own meaning and value. They are an expression of a great sagacity, even the supreme sagacity: where *nosce te ipsum* would be the recipe for destruction, self-forgetfulness, self-*misunderstanding*, self-diminution, -narrowing, -mediocratizing becomes reason itself. Expressed morally: love of one's neighbour, living for others and other things *can* be the defensive measure for the preservation of the sternest selfishness. This is the exceptional case in which I, contrary to my rule and conviction, take the side of the 'selfless' drives: here they work in the service of *selfishness*, *self-cultivation*. – The entire surface of consciousness – consciousness *is* a surface – has to be kept clear of any of the great imperatives. Even the grand words, the grand attitudes must be guarded against! All of them represent a danger that the instinct will 'understand itself' too early – –. In the meantime the organizing 'idea' destined to rule grows and grows in the depths – it begins to command, it slowly leads *back* from sidepaths and wrong turnings, it prepares *individual* qualities and abilities which will one day prove themselves indispensable as means to achieving the whole – it constructs the *ancillary* capacities one after the other before it gives any hint of the dominating task, of the 'goal', 'objective', 'meaning'. – Regarded from this side my life is simply wonderful. For the task of a *revaluation of values* more capacities perhaps were required than have dwelt together in one individual, above all antithetical capacities which however are not allowed to disturb or destroy one another. Order of rank among capacities; distance; the art of dividing without making inimical; mixing up nothing, 'reconciling' nothing; a tremendous multiplicity which is none the less the opposite of chaos – this has been the precondition, the protracted secret labour and artistic working of my instinct. The magnitude of its *higher protection* was shown in the fact I have at no time had the remotest idea what was growing within me – that all my abilities one day *leapt forth* suddenly ripe, in their final perfection. I cannot remember ever having taken any trouble – no trace of *struggle* can be discovered in my life, I am the opposite of an heroic nature. To 'want' something, to 'strive' after something, to have a 'goal', a 'wish' in view – I know none of this from experience. Even at this moment I look out upon my future – a *distant* future! – as upon a smooth sea: it is ruffled by no desire. I do not want in the slightest that anything should become other than it is; I do not want myself to become other than I am . . . But that is how I have always lived. I have harboured no desire. Someone who after his forty-fourth year can say he has never striven after *honours*, after *women*, after *money*! – Not that I could not have had them . . . Thus, for example, I one day became a university professor – I had never had the remotest thought of such a thing, for I was barely twenty-four years old.

10

– I shall be asked why I have really narrated all these little things which according to the traditional judgement are matters of indifference: it will be said that in doing so I harm myself all the more if I am destined to fulfil great tasks. Answer: these little things – nutriment, place, climate, recreation, the whole casuistry of selfishness – are beyond all conception of greater importance than anything that has been considered of importance hitherto. It is precisely here that one has to begin to *learn anew*. Those things which mankind has hitherto pondered seriously are not even realities, merely imaginings, more strictly speaking *lies* from the bad instincts of sick, in the profoundest sense injurious natures – all the concepts 'God', 'soul', 'virtue', 'sin', 'the Beyond', 'truth', 'eternal life' . . . But the greatness of human nature, its 'divinity', has been sought in them . . . All questions of politics, the ordering of society, education have been falsified down to their foundations because the most injurious men have been taken for great men – because contempt has been taught for the 'little' things, which is to say for the fundamental affairs of life . . .

Now, when I compare myself with the men who have hitherto been honoured as *pre-eminent* men the distinction is palpable. I do not count these supposed 'pre-eminent men' as belonging to mankind at all – to me they are the refuse of mankind, abortive offspring of sickness and vengeful instincts: they are nothing but pernicious, fundamentally incurable monsters who take revenge on life . . . I want to be the antithesis of this: it is my privilege to possess the highest subtlety for all the signs of healthy instincts. Every morbid trait is lacking in me; even in periods of severe illness I did not become morbid; a trait of fanaticism will be sought in vain in my nature. At no moment of my life can I be shown to have adopted any kind of arrogant or pathetic posture. The pathos of attitudes does *not* belong to greatness; whoever needs attitudes at all is *false* . . . Beware of all picturesque men! – Life has been easy for me, easiest when it demanded of me the most difficult things. Anyone who saw me during the seventy days of this autumn when I was uninterruptedly creating nothing but things of the first rank which no man will be able to do again or has done before, bearing a responsibility for all the coming millennia, will have noticed no trace of tension in me, but rather an overflowing freshness and cheerfulness. I never ate with greater relish, I never slept better. – I know of no other way of dealing with great tasks than that of *play*: this is, as a sign of greatness, an essential precondition. The slightest constraint, the gloomy mien, any kind of harsh note in the throat are all objections to a man, how much more to his work! . . . One must have no nerves . . . To *suffer* from solitude is likewise an objection – I have always suffered only from the 'multi-tude' . . . At an absurdly early age, at the age of seven, I already knew that no human word would ever reach me: has anyone ever seen me sad on that account? – Still today I treat everyone with the same geniality, I am even full of consideration for the basest people: in all this there is not a grain of arrogance, of secret contempt. He whom I despise *divines* that I despise him: through my mere existence I enrage everything that has bad blood in its veins . . . My formula for greatness in a human being is *amor fati*: that one wants nothing to be other than it is, not in the future, not in the past, not in all eternity. Not merely to endure that which happens of necessity, still less to dissemble it – all idealism is untruthfulness in the face of necessity – but to *love* it . . .

Why I Write Such Good Books

I AM one thing, my writings are another. – Here, before I speak of these writings themselves, I shall touch on the question of their being understood or *not* understood. I shall do so as perfunctorily as is fitting: for the time for this question has certainly not yet come. My time has not yet come, some are born posthumously. – One day or other institutions will be needed in which people live and teach as I understand living and teaching: perhaps even chairs for the interpretation of Zarathustra will be established. But it would be a complete contradiction of myself if I expected ears *and hands* for *my* truths already today: that I am not heard today, that no one today knows how to take from me, is not only comprehensible; it even seems to me right. I do not want to be taken for what I am not – and that requires that I do not take myself for what I am not. To say it again, little of 'ill will' can be shown in my life; neither would I be able to speak of barely a single case of 'literary ill will'. On the other hand all too much of *pure folly*! . . . It seems to me that to take a book of mine into his hands is one of the rarest distinctions anyone can confer upon himself – I even assume he removes his shoes when he does so – not to speak of boots . . . When Doctor Heinrich von

Stein once honestly complained that he understood not one word of my Zarathustra, I told him that was quite in order: to have understood, that is to say *experienced*, six sentences of that book would raise one to a higher level of mortals than 'modern' man could attain to. How *could* I, with *this* feeling of distance, even want the 'modern men' I know – to read me! – My triumph is precisely the opposite of Schopenhauer's – I say 'non *legor*, non *legar*'. – Not that I should like to underestimate the pleasure which the *innocence* in the rejection of my writings has given me. This very summer just gone, at a time when, with my own weighty, too heavily weighty literature, I was perhaps throwing all the rest of literature off its balance, a professor of Berlin University kindly gave me to understand that I ought really to avail myself of a different form: no one read stuff like mine. – In the end it was not Germany but Switzerland which offered me the two extreme cases. An essay of Dr V. Widmann in the *Bund* on 'Beyond Good and Evil' under the title 'Nietzsche's Dangerous Book', and a general report on my books as a whole on the part of Herr Karl Spitteler, also in the *Bund*, constitute a maximum in my life – of what I take care not to say . . . The latter, for example, dealt with my Zarathustra as an *advanced exercise in style*, with the request that I might later try to provide some content; Dr Widmann expressed his respect for the courage with which I strive to abolish all decent feelings. – Through a little trick of chance every sentence here was, with a consistency I had to admire, a truth stood on its head: remarkably enough, all one had to do was to 'revalue all values' in order to hit the nail on the head with regard to me – instead of hitting my head with a nail . . . All the more reason for me to attempt an explanation. – Ultimately, no one can extract from things, books included, more than he already knows. What one has no access to through experience one has no ear for. Now let us imagine an extreme case: that a book speaks of nothing but events which lie outside the possibility of general or even of rare experience – that it is the *first* language for a new range of experiences. In this case simply nothing will be heard, with the acoustical illusion that where nothing is heard there *is* nothing . . . This is in fact my average experience and, if you like, the *originality* of my experience. Whoever believed he had understood something of me had dressed up something out of me after his own image – not uncommonly an antithesis of me, for instance an 'idealist'; whoever had understood nothing of me denied that I came into consideration at all. – The word 'superman' to designate a type that has turned out supremely well, in antithesis to 'modern' men, to 'good' men, to Christians and other nihilists – a word which, in the mouth of a Zarathustra, the *destroyer* of morality, becomes a very thoughtful word – has almost everywhere been understood with perfect innocence in the sense of those values whose antithesis makes its appearance in the figure of Zarathustra: that is to say as an 'idealistic' type of higher species of man, half 'saint', half 'genius' . . . Other learned cattle caused me on its account to be suspected of Darwinism; even the 'hero cult' of that great unconscious and involuntary counterfeiter Carlyle which I rejected so maliciously has been recognized in it. He into whose ear I whispered he ought to look around rather for a Cesare Borgia than for a Parsifal did not believe his ears. – That I am utterly incurious about discussions of my books, especially by newspapers, will have to be forgiven me. My friends, my publishers know this and do not speak to me about such things. In a particular instance I once had a sight of all the sins that had been committed against a single book – it was 'Beyond Good and Evil'; I could tell a pretty story about that. Would you believe it that the 'Nationalzeitung' – a Prussian newspaper, for my foreign readers – I myself read, if I may say so, only the Journal des Débats – could in all seriousness understand the book as a 'sign of the times', as the real genuine *Junker philosophy* for which the 'Kreuzzeitung' merely lacked the courage? . . .

2

This was said for Germans: for I have readers everywhere else – nothing but *choice* intelligences of proved character brought up in high positions and duties; I have even real geniuses among my readers. In Vienna, in St Petersburg, in Stockholm, in Copenhagen, in Paris and New York – I have been discovered everywhere: I have *not* been in Europe's flatland Germany . . . And to confess it, I rejoice even more over my non-readers, such as have never heard either my name or the word philosophy; but wherever I go, here in Turin for example, every face grows more cheerful and benevolent at the sight of me. What has flattered me the most is that old market-women take great pains to select together for me the sweetest of their grapes. That is *how far* one must be a philosopher . . . It is not in vain that the Poles are called the French among the Slavs. A charming Russian lady would not mistake for a moment where I belong. I cannot succeed in becoming solemn, the most I can achieve is embarrassment . . . To think German, to feel German – I can do everything, but *that* is beyond my powers . . . My old teacher Ritschl went so far as to maintain that I conceived even my philological essays like a Parisian *romancier* – absurdly exciting. In Paris itself there is astonishment over '*toutes mes audaces et finesses*' – the expression is Monsieur Taine's –; I fear that with me there is up to the highest forms of the dithyramb an admixture of that salt which never gets soggy – 'German' – *esprit* . . . I cannot do otherwise, so help me God! Amen. – We all know, some even know from experience, what a longears is. Very well, I dare to assert that I possess the smallest ears. This is of no little interest to women – it seems to me they feel themselves better understood by me? . . . I am the *anti-ass par excellence* and therewith a world-historical monster – I am, in Greek and not only in Greek, the *Anti-Christ* . . .

3

I know my privileges as a writer to some extent; in individual cases it has been put to me how greatly habituation to my writings 'ruins' taste. One can simply no longer endure other books, philosophical ones least of all. To enter this noble and delicate world is an incomparable distinction – to do so one absolutely must not be a German; it is in the end a distinction one has to have earned. But he who is related to me through *loftiness* of will experiences when he reads me real ecstasies of learning: for I come from heights no bird has ever soared to, I know abysses into which no foot has ever yet strayed. I have been told it is impossible to put a book of mine down – I even disturb the night's rest . . . There is altogether no prouder and at the same time more exquisite kind of book than my books – they attain here and there the highest thing that can be attained on earth, cynicism; one needs the most delicate fingers as well as the bravest fists if one is to master them. Any infirmity of soul excludes one from them once and for all, any dyspepsia, even, does so: one must have no nerves, one must have a joyful belly. Not only does the poverty, the hole-and-corner air of a soul exclude it from them – cowardice, uncleanliness, secret revengefulness in the entrails does so far more: a word from me drives all bad instincts into the face. I have among my acquaintances several experimental animals on whom I bring home to myself the various, very instructively various reactions to my writings. Those who want to have nothing to do with their contents, my so-called friends for example, become 'impersonal': they congratulate me on having 'done it' again – progress is apparent, too, in a greater cheerfulness of tone . . . The completely vicious 'spirits', the 'beautiful souls', the thoroughly and utterly men-dacious have no idea at all what to do with these books – consequently they see the same as *beneath* them, the beautiful consistency of all 'beautiful souls'. The horned cattle among my acquaintances, mere Germans if I may say so, give me to understand they are not always of my opinion, though they are sometimes . . . I have heard this said even of Zarathustra . . . Any 'feminism' in a person, or in a man, likewise closes the gates on me: one will never be able to enter this labyrinth of daring knowledge. One must never have spared oneself, *harshness* must be among one's habits, if one is to be happy and cheerful among nothing but hard truths. When I picture a perfect reader, I always picture a monster of courage and curiosity, also something supple, cunning, cautious, a born adventurer and discoverer. Finally: I would not know how to say better to whom at bottom alone I speak than Zarathustra has said it: *to whom* alone does he want to narrate his riddle?

To you, the bold venturers and adventurers, and whoever has embarked with cunning sails upon dreadful seas,

to you who are intoxicated with riddles, who take pleasure in twilight, whose soul is lured with flutes to every treacherous abyss –

for you do not desire to feel for a rope with cowardly hand; and where you can *guess* you hate to *calculate* . . .

4

I shall at the same time also say a general word on my *art of style*. To *communicate* a state, an inner tension of pathos through signs, including the tempo of these signs – that is the meaning of every style; and considering that the multiplicity of inner states is in my case extraordinary, there exists in my case the possibility of many styles – altogether the most manifold art of style any man has ever had at his disposal. Every style is *good* which actually communicates an inner state, which makes no mistake as to the signs, the tempo of the signs, the *gestures* – all rules of phrasing are art of gesture. My instinct is here infallible. – Good style *in itself* – a piece of pure folly, mere 'idealism', on a par with the 'beautiful *in itself*', the 'good *in itself*', the 'thing *in itself*' . . . Always presupposing there are ears – that there are those capable and worthy of a similar pathos, that those are not lacking to whom one *ought* to communicate oneself. – My Zarathustra for example is at present still looking for them – alas! he will have to look for a long time yet! One has to be *worthy* of assaying him . . . And until then there will be no one who comprehends the *art* which has here been squandered: no one has ever had more of the new, the unheard-of, the really new-created in artistic means to squander. That such a thing was possible in the German language remained to be proved: I myself would previously have most hotly disputed it. Before me one did not know what can be done with the German language – what can be done with language as such. The art of *grand* rhythm, the *grand style* of phrasing, as the expression of a tremendous rise and fall of sublime, of superhuman passion, was first discovered by me; with a dithyramb such as the last of the *third* Zarathustra, entitled 'The Seven Seals', I flew a thousand miles beyond that which has hitherto been called poesy.

5

That out of my writings there speaks a *psychologist* who has not his equal, that is perhaps the first thing a good reader will notice – a reader such as I deserve, who reads me as good old philologists read their Horace. The propositions over which everybody is in fundamental agreement – not to speak of everybody's philosophers, the moralists and other hollow-heads and cabbage-heads – appear with me as naive blunders: for example that belief that 'unegoistic' and 'egoistic' are antitheses, while the *ego* itself is merely a 'higher swindle', an 'ideal'. There are *neither* egoistic *nor* unegoistic actions: both concepts are psychologically nonsense. Or the proposition 'man strives after happiness' . . . Or the proposition 'happiness is the reward of virtue' . . . Or the proposition 'pleasure and displeasure are opposites' . . . The Circe of mankind, morality, has falsified all *psychologica* to its very foundations – has *moralized* it – to the point of the frightful absurdity that love is supposed to be something 'unegoistic' . . . One has to be set firmly upon *oneself*, one has to stand bravely upon one's own two legs, otherwise one *cannot* love at all. In the long run the little women know that all too well: they play the deuce with selfless, with merely objective men . . . Dare I venture in addition to suggest that I *know* these little women? It is part of my Dionysian endowment. Who knows? perhaps I am the first psychologist of the eternal-womanly. They all love me – an old story: excepting the *abortive* women, the 'emancipated' who lack the stuff for children. – Happily I am not prepared to be torn to pieces: the complete woman tears to pieces when she loves . . . I know these amiable maenads . . . Ah, what a dangerous, creeping, subterranean little beast of prey it is! And so pleasant with it! . . . A little woman chasing after her revenge would over-run fate itself. – The woman is unspeakably more wicked than the man, also cleverer;

goodness in a woman is already a form of *degeneration* . . . At the bottom of all so-called 'beautiful souls' there lies a physiological disadvantage – I shall not say all I could or I should become medicynical. The struggle for *equal* rights is even a symptom of sickness: every physician knows that. – The more a woman is a woman the more she defends herself tooth and nail against rights in general: for the state of nature, the eternal *war* between the sexes puts her in a superior position by far. – Have there been ears for my definition of love? it is the only one worthy of a philosopher. Love – in its methods war, in its foundation the mortal hatred of the sexes. Has my answer been heard to the question how one cures – 'redeems' – a woman? One makes a child for her. The woman has need of children, the man is always only the means: thus spoke Zarathustra. – 'Emancipation of woman' – is the instinctive hatred of the woman who has *turned out ill*, that is to say is incapable of bearing, for her who has turned out well – the struggle against 'man' is always only means, subterfuge, tactic. When they elevate *themselves* as 'woman in herself', as 'higher woman', as 'idealist' woman, they want to *lower* the general level of rank of woman; no surer means for achieving that than grammar school education, trousers and the political rights of voting cattle. At bottom the emancipated are the *anarchists* in the world of the 'eternal-womanly', the under-privileged whose deepest instinct is revenge . . . An entire species of the most malevolent 'idealism' – which, by the way, also occurs in men, for example in the case of Henrik Ibsen, that typical old maid – has the objective of *poisoning* the good conscience, the naturalness in sexual love . . . And so as to leave no doubt as to my opinion in this matter, which is as honest as it is strict, I would like to impart one more clause of my moral code against *vice*: with the word vice I combat every sort of anti-nature or, if one likes beautiful words, idealism. The clause reads: 'The preaching of chastity is a public incitement to anti-nature. Every expression of contempt for the sexual life, every befouling of it through the concept "impure", is *the* crime against life – is the intrinsic sin against the holy spirit of life.'

6

To give an idea of me as a psychologist I take a curious piece of psychology which occurs in 'Beyond Good and Evil' – I forbid, by the way, any conjecture as to whom I am describing in this passage: 'The genius of the heart as it is possessed by that great hidden one, the tempter god and born pied piper of consciences whose voice knows how to descend into the underworld of every soul, who says no word and gives no glance in which there lies no touch of enticement, to whose mastery belongs knowing how to seem – not what he is but what to those who follow him is one constraint *more* to press ever closer to him, to follow him ever more inwardly and thoroughly . . . The genius of the heart who makes everything loud and self-satisfied fall silent and teaches it to listen, who smooths rough souls and gives them a new desire to savour – the desire to lie still as a mirror, that the deep sky may mirror itself in them . . . The genius of the heart who teaches the stupid and hasty hand to hesitate and grasp more delicately; who divines the hidden and forgotten treasure, the drop of goodness and sweet spirituality under thick and opaque ice, and is a divining-rod for every grain of gold which has lain long in the prison of much mud and sand . . . The genius of the heart from whose touch everyone goes away richer, not favoured and surprised, not as if blessed and oppressed with the goods of others, but richer in himself, newer to himself than before, broken open, blown upon and sounded out by a thawing wind, more uncertain perhaps, more delicate, more fragile, more broken, but full of hopes that as yet have no names, full of new will and current, full of new ill will and counter current . . .'

Why I am a Destiny

I KNOW my fate. One day there will be associated with my name the recollection of something frightful – of a crisis like no other before on earth, of the profoundest collision of conscience, of a decision evoked *against* everything that until then had been believed in, demanded, sanctified. I am not a man, I am dynamite. – And with all that there is nothing in me of a founder of a religion – religions are affairs of the rabble, I have need of washing my hands after contact with religious people . . . I do not *want* 'believers', I think I am too malicious to believe in myself, I never speak to masses . . . I have a terrible fear I shall one day be pronounced *holy*: one will guess why I bring out this book *beforehand*; it is intended to prevent people from making mischief with me . . . I do not want to be a saint, rather even a buffoon . . . Perhaps I am a buffoon . . . And none the less, or rather *not* none the less – for there has hitherto been nothing more mendacious than saints – the truth speaks out of me. – But my truth is *dreadful*: for hitherto the *lie* has been called truth. – *Revaluation of all values*: this is my formula for an act of supreme coming-to-oneself on the part of mankind which in me has become flesh and genius. It is my fate to have to be the first *decent* human

being, to know myself in opposition to the mendaciousness of millennia . . . I was the first to *discover* the
truth, in that I was the first to sense – *smell* – the lie as
lie . . . My genius is in my nostrils . . . I contradict as
has never been contradicted and am none the less the
opposite of a negative spirit. I am a *bringer of good tidings*
such as there has never been, I know tasks from such a
height that any conception of them has hitherto been
lacking; only after me is it possible to hope again. With
all that I am necessarily a man of fatality. For when truth
steps into battle with the lie of millennia we shall have
convulsions, an earthquake spasm, a transposition of
valley and mountain such as has never been dreamed
of. The concept politics has then become completely
absorbed into a war of spirits; all the power-structures
of the old society have been blown into the air – they
one and all reposed on the lie: there will be wars such as
there have never yet been on earth. Only after me will
there be *grand politics* on earth.

2

Does one want a formula for a destiny *that has become
man?* It stands in my Zarathustra.

*– and he who wants to be a creator in good and evil has first
to be a destroyer and break values.*

*Thus the greatest evil belongs with the greatest good: this,
however, is the creative good.*

I am by far the most terrible human being there has
ever been; this does not mean I shall not be the most

beneficent. I know joy in *destruction* to a degree corre-
sponding to my *strength* for destruction – in both I obey
my dionysian nature, which does not know how to
separate No-doing from Yes-saying. I am the first
immoralist: I am therewith the *destroyer par excellence*. –

3

I have not been asked, as I should have been asked, what
the name Zarathustra means in precisely my mouth,
in the mouth of the first immoralist: for what constitutes
the tremendous uniqueness of that Persian in history is
precisely the opposite of this. Zarathustra was the first
to see in the struggle between good and evil the actual
wheel in the working of things: the translation of morality into the realm of metaphysics, as force, cause, end-in-
itself, is *his* work. But this question is itself at bottom its
own answer. Zarathustra *created* this most fateful of
errors, morality: consequently he must also be the first
to *recognize* it. Not only has he had longer and greater
experience here than any other thinker – the whole
of history is indeed the experimental refutation of the
proposition of a so-called 'moral world-order' –: what is
more important is that Zarathustra is more truthful than
any other thinker. His teaching, and his alone, upholds
truthfulness as the supreme virtue – that is to say, the
opposite of the *cowardice* of the 'idealist', who takes flight
in face of reality; Zarathustra has more courage in him
than all other thinkers put together. To tell the truth and
to shoot well with arrows: that is Persian virtue. – Have
I been understood? The self-overcoming of morality
through truthfulness, the self-overcoming of the moralist

into his opposite – *into me* – that is what the name
Zarathustra means in my mouth.

4

At bottom my expression *immoralist* involves two
denials. I deny first a type of man who has hitherto
counted as the highest, the *good*, the *benevolent, beneficent*;
I deny secondly a kind of morality which has come to be
accepted and to dominate as morality in itself – *décadence*
morality, in more palpable terms *Christian* morality. The
second contradiction might be seen as the decisive one,
since the over-valuation of goodness and benevolence
by and large already counts with me as a consequence
of *décadence*, as a symptom of weakness, as incompatible
with an ascending and affirmative life: denial *and destruction* is a condition of affirmation. – I deal first of all with
the psychology of the good man. In order to assess what
a type of man is worth one has to compute how much
his preservation costs – one has to know the conditions
of his existence. The condition for the existence of the
good is the *lie* –: expressed differently, the *desire* not to
see at any price what is the fundamental constitution of
reality, that is to say *not* such as to call forth benevolent
instincts at all times, even less such as to permit at
all times an interference by short-sighted good-natured
hands. To regard *states of distress* in general as an objection, as something that must be *abolished*, is the *niaiserie
par excellence*, in a general sense a real disaster in its
consequences, a fatality of stupidity – almost as stupid as
would be the will to abolish bad weather – perhaps from
pity to the poor . . . In the general economy of the whole

the fearfulnesses of reality (in the affects, in the desires, in the will to power) are to an incalculable degree more necessary than any form of petty happiness, so-called 'goodness'; since the latter is conditioned by falsity of instinct one must even be cautious about granting it a place at all. I shall have a grand occasion of demonstrating the measurelessly uncanny consequences for the whole of history of *optimism*, that offspring of the *homines optimi*. Zarathustra, the first to grasp that optimism is just as *décadent* as pessimism and perhaps more harmful, says: *good men never tell the truth. The good taught you false shores and false securities: you were born and kept in the lies of the good. Everything has been distorted and twisted down to its very bottom through the good.* Fortunately the world has not been constructed for the satisfaction of instincts such as would permit merely good-natured herd animals to find their narrow happiness in it; to demand that everything should become 'good man', herd animal, blue-eyed, benevolent, 'beautiful soul' – or, as Mr Herbert Spencer wants, altruistic, would mean to deprive existence of its *great* character, would mean to castrate mankind and to reduce it to a paltry Chinadom. – *And this has been attempted!* . . . *Precisely this has been called morality* . . . In this sense Zarathustra calls the good now 'the last men', now the 'beginning of the end'; above all he feels them to be the *most harmful species of man*, because they preserve their existence as much at the expense of *truth* as at the expense of the *future.*

The good – cannot *create*, they are always the beginning of the end –

– they crucify him who writes *new* values on new law-tables, they sacrifice the future *to themselves*, they crucify the whole human future!

The good – have always been the beginning of the end . . .

And whatever harm the world-calumniators may do, *the harm the good do is the most harmful harm.*

5

Zarathustra, the first psychologist of the good, is – consequently – a friend of the wicked. When a *décadence*-species of man has risen to the rank of the highest species of man, this can happen only at the expense of its antithetical species, the species of man strong and certain of life. When the herd-animal is resplendent in the glow of the highest virtue, the exceptional man must be devalued to the wicked man. When mendaciousness at any price appropriates the word 'truth' for its perspective, what is actually veracious must be discovered bearing the worst names. Zarathustra here leaves no doubt: he says that it was knowledge of precisely the good, the 'best', which made him feel horror at man in general; it was out of *this* repugnance that the wings grew which 'carried him to distant futures' – he does not dissemble that it is precisely in relation to the *good* that *his* type of man, a relatively superhuman type, is superhuman, that the good and just would call his superman a *devil* . . .

You highest men my eyes have encountered! This is my doubt of you and my secret laughter: I think you would call my superman – a devil!

Your souls are so unfamiliar with what is great that the superman would be *fearful* to you in his *goodness* . . .

It is at this point and nowhere else that one must make a start if one is to understand what Zarathustra's intentions are: the species of man he delineates delineates reality *as it is*: he is strong enough for it – he is not estranged from or entranced by it, he is *reality itself*, he still has all that is fearful and questionable in reality in him, *only thus can man possess greatness* . . .

6

– But there is also another sense in which I have chosen for myself the word *immoralist* as a mark of distinction and badge of honour; I am proud to possess this word which sets me off against the whole of humanity. No one has yet felt *Christian* morality as *beneath* him: that requires a height, a farsightedness, a hitherto altogether unheard-of psychological profundity and abysmalness. Christian morality has hitherto been the Circe of all thinkers – they stood in its service. – Who before me has entered the caverns out of which the poisonous blight of this kind of ideal – *world-calumny!* – wells up? Who has even ventured to suspect *that* these caverns exist? Who before me at all among philosophers has been a *psychologist* and not rather its opposite 'higher swindler', 'idealist'? Before me there was no psychology. – To be the first here can be a curse, it is in any case a destiny: *for one is also the first to despise* . . . *Disgust* at mankind is my danger . . .

7

Have I been understood? – What defines me, what sets me apart from all the rest of mankind, is that I have *unmasked* Christian morality. That is why I needed a word which would embody the sense of a challenge to everyone. Not to have opened its eyes here sooner counts to me as the greatest piece of uncleanliness which humanity has on its conscience, as self-deception become instinct, as a fundamental will *not* to observe every event, every cause, every reality, as false-coinage *in psychologicis* to the point of crime. Blindness in the face of Christianity is the *crime par excellence* – the crime *against life* . . . The millennia, the peoples, the first and the last, the philosophers and the old women – except for five or six moments of history, me as the seventh – on this point they are all worthy of one another. The Christian has hitherto been *the* 'moral being', a curiosity without equal – and, *as* 'moral being', more absurd, mendacious, vain, frivolous, *harmful to himself* than even the greatest despiser of mankind could have allowed himself to dream. Christian morality – the most malicious form of the will to the lie, the actual Circe of mankind: that which has *ruined* it. It is *not* error as error which horrifies me at the sight of this, *not* the millennia-long lack of 'good will', of discipline, of decency, of courage in spir-itual affairs which betrays itself in its victory – it is the lack of nature, it is the utterly ghastly fact that *anti-nature* itself has received the highest honours as morality, and has hung over mankind as law, as categorical imperative! . . . To blunder to this extent, *not* as an individual, *not* as a people, but as mankind! . . . That contempt has been taught for the primary instincts of life; that a 'soul', a 'spirit' has been *lyingly invented* in order to destroy the body; that one teaches that there is something unclean in the precondition of life, sexuality; that the evil principle is sought in that which is most profoundly necessary for prosperity, in *strict* selfishness (– the very word is slanderous!); that on the other hand one sees in the typical signs of decline and contradictoriness of instinct, in the 'selfless', in loss of centre of gravity, in 'depersonalization' and 'love of one's neighbour' (– *lust for* one's neighbour!) the *higher* value, what am I saying! *value in itself*! . . . *What*! could mankind itself be in *décadence*? has it always been? – What is certain is that it has been *taught* only *décadence* values as supreme values. The morality of unselfing is the morality of decline *par excellence*, the fact 'I am perishing' translated into the imperative 'you all *shall* perish' – and *not only* into the imperative! . . . This sole morality which has hitherto been taught, the morality of unselfing, betrays a will to the end, it *denies* the very foundations of life. – Let us here leave the possibility open that it is not mankind which is degenerating but only that parasitic species of man the *priest*, who with the aid of morality has lied himself up to being the determiner of mankind's values – who divines in Christian morality his means to *power* . . . And that is in fact *my* insight: the teachers, the leaders of mankind, theologians included, have also one and all been *décadents: thence* the revaluation of all values into the inimical to life, *thence* morality . . . *Definition of morality*: morality – the idiosyncrasy of *décadents* with the hidden intention of *avenging themselves on life – and* successfully. I set store by *this* definition.

8

– Have I been understood? – I have not just now said a word that I could not have said five years ago through the mouth of Zarathustra. – The *unmasking* of Christian morality is an event without equal, a real catastrophe. He who exposes it is a *force majeure*, a destiny – he breaks the history of mankind into two parts. One lives *before* him, one lives *after* him . . . The lightning-bolt of truth struck precisely that which formerly stood highest: he who grasps *what* was then destroyed had better see whether he has anything at all left in his hands. Everything hitherto called 'truth' is recognized as the most harmful, malicious, most subterranean form of the lie; the holy pretext of 'improving' mankind as the cunning to *suck out* life itself and to make it anaemic. Morality as *vampirism* . . . He who unmasks morality has therewith unmasked the valuelessness of all values which are or have been believed in; he no longer sees in the most revered, even *canonized* types of man anything venerable, he sees in them the most fateful kind of abortion, fateful *because they exercise fascination* . . . The concept 'God' invented as the antithetical concept to life – everything harmful, noxious, slanderous, the whole mortal enmity against life brought into one terrible unity! The concept 'the Beyond', 'real world' invented so as to deprive of value the *only* world which exists – so as to leave over no goal, no reason, no task for our earthly reality! The concept 'soul', 'spirit', finally even 'immortal soul', invented so as to despise the body, so as to make it sick – 'holy' – so as to bring to all the things in life which deserve serious attention, the questions of nutriment, residence, cleanliness, weather, a horrifying frivolity! Instead of health 'salvation of the soul' – which is to say a *folie circulaire* between spasms of atonement and redemption hysteria! The concept 'sin' invented together with the instrument of torture which goes with it, the concept of 'free will', so as to confuse the instincts, so as to make mistrust of the instincts into second nature! In the concept of the 'selfless', of the 'self-denying' the actual badge of *décadence*, being *lured* by the harmful, no longer being *able* to discover where one's advantage lies, self-destruction, made the sign of value in general, made 'duty', 'holiness', the 'divine' in man! Finally – it is the most fearful – in the concept of the *good* man common cause made with everything weak, sick, ill-constructed, suffering from itself, all that *which ought to perish* – the law of *selection* crossed, an ideal made of opposition to the proud and well-constituted, to the affirmative man, to the man certain of the future and guaranteeing the future – the latter is henceforth called the *evil man* . . . And all this was believed in *as morality*! – *Ecrasez l'infâme!* –

9

– Have I been understood? – *Dionysos against the Crucified* . . .

Twilight of the Idols

or How to Philosophize with a Hammer

Maxims and Arrows

1. Idleness is the beginning of psychology. What? could psychology be – a vice?

2. Even the bravest of us rarely has the courage for what he really *knows* . . .

3. To live alone one must be an animal or a god – says Aristotle. There is yet a third case: one must be both – a *philosopher.*

4. 'All truth is simple' – Is that not a compound lie? –

5. Once and for all, there is a great deal I do *not* want to know. – Wisdom sets bounds even to knowledge.

6. It is by being 'natural' that one best recovers from one's unnaturalness, from one's spirituality . . .

7. Which is it? Is man only God's mistake or God only man's mistake? –

8. *From the military school of life* – What does not kill me makes me stronger.

9. Help thyself: then everyone will help thee too. Principle of Christian charity.

10. Let us not be cowardly in face of our actions! Let

us not afterwards leave them in the lurch! – Remorse of conscience is indecent.

11. Can an *ass* be tragic? – To be crushed by a burden one can neither bear nor throw off? . . . The case of the philosopher.

12. If we possess our *why* of life we can put up with almost any *how*. – Man does *not* strive after happiness; only the Englishman does that.

13. Man created woman – but what out of? Out of a rib of his God, of his 'ideal' . . .

14. What? you are seeking? you want to multiply yourself by ten, by a hundred? you are seeking followers? – Seek *noughts*!

15. Posthumous men – like me, for instance – are not so well understood as timely men, but they are *listened to* better. More precisely: we are never understood – and *hence* our authority . . .

16. *Among women*. – 'Truth? Oh, you don't know the truth, do you! Is it not an outrage on all our *pudeurs*?' –

17. This is an artist as an artist should be, modest in his requirements: there are only two things he really wants, his bread and his art – *panem et* Circen . . .

18. He who does not know how to put his will into things at least puts a *meaning* into them: that is, he believes there is a will in them already (principle of 'belief').

19. What? you have chosen virtue and the heaving bosom, yet at the same time look with envy on the advantages enjoyed by those who live for the day? – But with virtue one *renounces* 'advantage' . . . (laid at the door of an anti-Semite).

20. The complete woman perpetrates literature in the same way as she perpetrates a little sin: as an experiment, in passing, looking around to see if someone notices and *so that* someone may notice . . .

21. To get into only those situations in which illusory virtues are of no use, but in which, like the tightrope-walker on his rope, one either falls or stands – or gets off . . .

22. 'Bad men have no songs' – How is it the Russians have songs?

23. 'German spirit': for eighteen years a *contradictio in adjecta*.

24. In order to look for beginners one becomes a crab. The historian looks backwards; at last he also *believes* backwards.

25. Contentment protects one even from catching a cold. Has a woman who knew she was well dressed ever caught a cold? – I am assuming she was hardly dressed at all.

26. I mistrust all systematizers and avoid them. The will to a system is a lack of integrity.

27. Women are considered deep – why? because one can never discover any bottom to them. Women are not even shallow.

28. If a woman possesses manly virtues one should run away from her; and if she does not possess them she runs away herself.

29. 'How much the conscience formerly had to bite on! what good teeth it had! – And today? what's the trouble?' – A dentist's question.

30. One seldom commits only one rash act. In the first rash act one always does too much. For just that reason one usually commits a second – and then one does too little . . .

31. When it is trodden on a worm will curl up. That is prudent. It thereby reduces the chance of being trodden on again. In the language of morals: *humility.* –

32. Hatred of lies and dissembling may arise out of a sensitive notion of honour; the same hatred may arise out of cowardice, in as much as lying is *forbidden* by divine command. Too cowardly to tell lies . . .

33. How little is needed for happiness! The note of a bagpipe. – Without music life would be a mistake. The German even thinks of God as singing songs.

34. *On ne peut penser et écrire qu' assis* (G. Flaubert). – Now I have you, nihilist! Assiduity is the *sin* against the holy spirit. Only ideas *won by walking* have any value.

35. There are times when we are like horses, we psychologists, and grow restive: we see our own shadow moving up and down before us. The psychologist has to look away from *himself* in order to see at all.

36. Whether we immoralists do virtue any *harm*? – As little as anarchists do princes. Only since they have been shot at do they again sit firmly on their thrones. Moral: one must shoot at morals.

37. You run on *ahead*? – Do you do so as a herdsman? or as an exception? A third possibility would be as a deserter . . . *First* question of conscience.

38. Are you genuine? or only an actor? A representative? or that itself which is represented? – Finally you are no more than an imitation of an actor . . . *Second* question of conscience.

39. *The disappointed man speaks.* – I sought great human beings, I never found anything but the *apes* of their ideal.

40. Are you one who looks on? or who sets to work? – or who looks away, turns aside . . . *Third* question of conscience.

41. Do you want to accompany? or go on ahead? or go off alone? . . . One must know *what* one wants and *that* one wants. – *Fourth* question of conscience.

42. For me they were steps, I have climbed up upon them – therefore I had to pass over them. But they thought I wanted to settle down on them . . .

43. What does it matter that *I* am proved right! I *am* too much in the right. – And he who laughs best today will also laugh last.

44. Formula of my happiness; a Yes, a No, a straight line, a *goal* . . .

The Four Great Errors

I

The error of confusing cause and consequence. – There is no more dangerous error than that of *mistaking the consequence for the cause*: I call it reason's intrinsic form of corruption. None the less, this error is among the most ancient and most recent habits of mankind: it is even sanctified among us, it bears the names 'religion' and 'morality'. *Every* proposition formulated by religion and morality contains it, priests and moral legislators are the authors of this corruption of reason. – I adduce an example. Everyone knows the book of the celebrated Cornaro in which he recommends his meagre diet as a recipe for a long and happy life – a virtuous one, too. Few books have been so widely read; even now many thousands of copies are printed in England every year. I do not doubt that hardly any book (the Bible rightly excepted) has done so much harm, has shortened so many lives, as this curiosity, which was so well meant. The reason: mistaking the consequence for the cause. The worthy Italian saw in his diet the *cause* of his long life: while the prerequisite of long life, an extraordinarily slow metabolism, a small consumption, was the cause of his meagre diet. He was not free to eat much *or* little as he chose, his frugality was *not* an act of 'free will': he became ill when he ate more. But if one is not a bony fellow of this sort one does not merely do well, one positively needs to eat *properly*. A scholar of *our* day, with his rapid consumption of nervous energy, would kill himself with Cornaro's regimen. *Credo experto*. –

2

The most general formula at the basis of every religion and morality is: 'Do this and this, refrain from this and this – and you will be happy! Otherwise . . .' Every morality, every religion *is* this imperative – I call it the great original sin of reason, *immortal unreason*. In my mouth this formula is converted into its reverse – *first* example of my 'revaluation of all values': a well-constituted human being, a 'happy one', *must* perform certain actions and instinctively shrinks from other actions, he transports the order of which he is the physiological representative into his relations with other human beings and with things. In a formula: his virtue is the *consequence* of his happiness . . . Long life, a plentiful posterity is *not* the reward of virtue, virtue itself is rather just that slowing down of the metabolism which also has, among other things, a long life, a plentiful posterity, in short *Cornarism*, as its outcome. – The Church and morality say: 'A race, a people perishes through vice and luxury'. My *restored* reason says: when a people is perishing, degenerating physiologically, vice and luxury (that is to say the necessity for stronger and stronger and more and more frequent stimulants, such as every exhausted nature is acquainted with) *follow* therefrom. A young man grows prematurely pale and faded. His friends say: this and that illness is to blame. I say: *that* he became ill, *that* he failed to resist the illness, was already the consequence of an impoverished life, an hereditary exhaustion. The newspaper reader says: this party will ruin itself if it makes errors like this. My *higher* politics says: a party which makes errors like this is already finished – it is no longer secure in its instincts. Every error, of whatever kind, is a consequence of degeneration of instinct, disgregation of will: one has thereby virtually defined the *bad*. Everything *good* is instinct – and consequently easy, necessary, free. Effort is an objection, the *god* is typically distinguished from the hero (in my language: *light* feet are the first attribute of divinity).

3

The error of a false causality. – We have always believed we know what a cause is: but whence did we derive our knowledge, more precisely our belief we possessed this knowledge? From the realm of the celebrated 'inner facts', none of which has up till now been shown to be factual. We believed ourselves to be causal agents in the act of willing; we at least thought we were there *catching causality in the act*. It was likewise never doubted that all the *antecedentia* of an action, its causes, were to be sought in the consciousness and could be discovered there if one sought them – as 'motives': for otherwise one would not have been *free* to perform it, *responsible* for it. Finally, who would have disputed that a thought is caused? that the ego causes the thought? . . . Of these three 'inner facts' through which causality seemed to be guaranteed the first and most convincing was that of *will as cause*;

the conception of a consciousness ('mind') as cause and later still that of the ego (the 'subject') as cause are merely after-products after causality had, on the basis of will, been firmly established as a given fact, as *empiricism* . . . Meanwhile, we have thought better. Today we do not believe a word of it. The 'inner world' is full of phantoms and false lights: the will is one of them. The will no longer moves anything, consequently no longer explains anything – it merely accompanies events, it can also be absent. The so-called 'motive': another error. Merely a surface phenomenon of consciousness, an accompaniment to an act, which conceals rather than exposes the *antecedentia* of the act. And as for the ego! It has become a fable, a fiction, a play on words: it has totally ceased to think, to feel and to will! . . . What follows from this? There are no spiritual causes at all! The whole of the alleged empiricism which affirmed them has gone to the devil! *That* is what follows! – And we had made a nice misuse of that 'empiricism', we had *created* the world on the basis of it as a world of causes, as a world of will, as a world of spirit. The oldest and longest-lived psychology was at work here – indeed it has done nothing else: every event was to it an action, every action the effect of a will, the world became for it a multiplicity of agents, an agent ('subject') foisted itself upon every event. Man projected his three 'inner facts', that in which he believed more firmly than in anything else, will, spirit, ego, outside himself – he derived the concept 'being' only from the concept 'ego', he posited 'things' as possessing being according to his own image, according to his concept of the ego as cause. No wonder he later always discovered in things only *that which he had put into them!* – The thing itself, to say it again, the concept 'thing' is merely a reflection of the belief in the ego as cause ... And even your atom, *messieurs* mechanists and physicists, how much error, how much rudimentary psychology, still remains in your atom! – To say nothing of the 'thing in itself', that *horrendum pudendum* of the metaphysicians! The error of spirit as cause mistaken for reality! And made the measure of reality! And called *God*! –

4

The error of imaginary causes. – To start from the dream: on to a certain sensation, the result for example of a distant cannon-shot, a cause is subsequently foisted (often a whole little novel in which precisely the dreamer is the chief character). The sensation, meanwhile, continues to persist, as a kind of resonance: it waits, as it were, until the cause-creating drive permits it to step into the foreground – now no longer as a chance occurrence but as 'meaning'. The cannon-shot enters in a *causal* way, in an apparent inversion of time. That which comes later, the motivation, is experienced first, often with a hundred details which pass like lightning, the shot *follows* ... What has happened? The ideas *engendered* by a certain condition have been misunderstood as the cause of that condition. – We do just the same thing, in fact, when we are awake. Most of our general feelings – every sort of restraint, pressure, tension, explosion in the play and counter-play of our organs, likewise and especially the condition of the *nervus sympathicus* – excite our cause-creating drive; we want to have a *reason* for feeling *as we do* – for feeling well or for feeling ill. It never suffices us simply to establish the mere fact *that* we feel as we do: we acknowledge this fact – become *conscious* of it – only *when* we have furnished it with a motivation of some kind. – The memory, which in such a case becomes active without our being aware of it, calls up earlier states of a similar kind and the causal interpretations which have grown out of them – *not* their causality. To be sure, the belief that these ideas, the accompanying occurrences in the consciousness, were causes is also brought up by the memory. Thus there arises an *habituation* to a certain causal interpretation which in truth obstructs and even prohibits an *investigation* of the cause.

5

Psychological explanation. – To trace something unknown back to something known is alleviating, soothing, gratifying and gives moreover a feeling of power. Danger, disquiet, anxiety attend the unknown – the first instinct is to *eliminate* these distressing states. First principle: any explanation is better than none. Because it is at bottom only a question of wanting to get rid of oppressive ideas, one is not exactly particular about what means one uses to get rid of them: the first idea which explains that the unknown is in fact the known does so much good that one 'holds it for true'. Proof by *pleasure* ('by potency') as criterion of truth. – The cause-creating drive is thus conditioned and excited by the feeling of fear. The question 'why?' should furnish, if at all possible, not so much the cause for its own sake as a *certain kind of cause* – a soothing, liberating, alleviating cause. That something already *known*, experienced, inscribed in the memory is posited as cause is the first consequence of this need. The new, the unexperienced, the strange is excluded from being cause. – Thus there is sought not only some kind of explanation as cause, but a *selected* and *preferred* kind of explanation, the kind by means of which the feeling of the strange, new, unexperienced is most speedily and most frequently abolished – the *most common* explanations. – Consequence: a particular kind of cause-ascription comes to preponderate more and more, becomes concentrated into a system and finally comes to *dominate* over the rest, that is to say simply to exclude *other* causes and explanations. – The banker thinks at once of 'business', the Christian of 'sin', the girl of her love.

6

The entire realm of morality and religion falls under this concept of imaginary causes. – 'Explanation' of *unpleasant* general feelings. They arise from beings hostile to us (evil spirits: most celebrated case – hysterics misunderstood as witches). They arise from actions we cannot approve of (the feeling of 'sin', of 'culpability' foisted upon a physiological discomfort – one always finds reasons for being discontented with oneself). They arise as punishments, as payment for something we should not have done, should not have *been* (generalized in an impudent form by Schopenhauer into a proposition in which morality appears for what it is, the actual poisoner and calumniator of life: 'Every great pain, whether physical or mental, declares what it is we deserve; for it could not have come upon us if we had not deserved it.' *World as Will and Idea* II 666). They arise as the consequences of rash actions which have turned out badly (– the emotions, the senses assigned as 'cause', as 'to blame'; physiological states of distress construed, with the aid of *other* states of distress, as 'deserved'). – 'Explanation' of *pleasant* general feelings. They arise from trust in God. They arise from the consciousness of good actions (the so-called 'good conscience', a physiological condition sometimes so like a sound digestion as to be mistaken for it). They arise from the successful outcome of under-takings (– naïve fallacy: the successful outcome of an undertaking certainly does not produce any pleasant general feelings in a hypochondriac or a Pascal). They arise from faith, hope and charity – the Christian virtues. – In reality all these supposed explanations are *consequen-tial* states and as it were translations of pleasurable and unpleasurable feelings into a false dialect: one is in a state in which one can experience hope *because* the physiologi-cal basic feeling is once more strong and ample; one trusts in God *because* the feeling of plenitude and strength makes one calm. – Morality and religion fall entirely under the *psychology of error*: in every single case cause is mistaken for effect; or the effect of what is *believed* true is mistaken for the truth; or a state of consciousness is mistaken for the causation of this state.

7

The error of free will. – We no longer have any sympathy today with the concept of 'free will': we know only too well what it is – the most infamous of all the arts of the theologian for making mankind 'accountable' in his sense of the word, that is to say for *making mankind dependent on him* . . . I give here only the psychology of making men accountable. – Everywhere accountability is sought, it is usually the instinct for *punishing and judging* which seeks it. One has deprived becoming of its innocence if being in this or that state is traced back to will, to intentions, to accountable acts: the doctrine of will has been invented essentially for the purpose of punishment, that is of *finding guilty*. The whole of the old-style psychology, the psychology of will, has as its precondition the desire of its authors, the priests at the head of the ancient communities, to create for themselves a *right* to ordain punishments – or their desire to create for God a right to do so . . . Men were thought of as 'free' so that they could become *guilty*: consequently, every action *had* to be thought of as willed, the origin of every action as lying in the consciousness (– whereby the most *fundamental* falsification *in psychologicis* was made into the very principle of psychology) . . . Today, when we have started to move in the *reverse* direction, when we immoralists especially are trying with all our might to remove the concept of guilt and the concept of punishment from the world and to purge psychology, history, nature, the social institutions and sanctions of them, there is in our eyes no more radical opposition than that of the theologians, who continue to infect the innocence of becoming with 'punishment' and 'guilt' by means of the concept of the 'moral world-order'. Christianity is a hangman's metaphysics . . .

8

What alone can *our* teaching be? – That no one *gives* a human being his qualities: not God, not society, not his parents or ancestors, not *he himself* (– the nonsensical idea here last rejected was propounded, as 'intelligible freedom', by Kant, and perhaps also by Plato before him). *No one* is accountable for existing at all, or for being constituted as he is, or for living in the circumstances and surroundings in which he lives. The fatality of his nature cannot be disentangled from the fatality of all that which has been and will be. He is *not* the result of a special design, a will, a purpose; he is *not* the subject of an attempt to attain to an 'ideal of man' or an 'ideal of happiness' or an 'ideal of morality' – it is absurd to want to *hand over* his nature to some purpose or other. *We* invented the concept 'purpose': in reality purpose is *lacking* . . . One is necessary, one is a piece of fate, one belongs to the whole, one *is* in the whole – there exists nothing which could judge, measure, compare, condemn our being, for that would be to judge, measure, compare, condemn the whole . . . *But nothing exists apart from the whole!* – That no one is any longer made accountable, that the kind of being manifested cannot be traced back to a *causa prima*, that the world is a unity neither as sensorium nor as 'spirit', *this alone is the great liberation* – thus alone is the *innocence* of becoming restored . . . The concept 'God' has hitherto been the greatest *objection* to existence . . . We deny God; in denying God, we deny accountability: only by doing *that* do we redeem the world. –

The Hammer Speaks

'Why so hard?' the charcoal once said to the diamond; 'for are we not close relations?'

Why so soft? O my brothers, thus I ask you: for are you not – my brothers?

Why so soft, unresisting and yielding? Why is there so much denial and abnegation in your hearts? So little fate in your glances?

And if you will not be fates, if you will not be inexorable: how can you – conquer with me?

And if your hardness will not flash and cut and cut to pieces: how can you one day – create with me?

For all creators are hard. And it must seem bliss to you to press your hand upon millennia as upon wax,

bliss to write upon the will of millennia as upon metal – harder than metal, nobler than metal. Only the noblest is perfectly hard.

This new law-table do I put over you, O my brothers: Become hard!